D0912189

Centripetal Worship

The Evangelical Heart of Lutheran Worship

Edited by
Timothy J. Wengert

Augsburg Fortress

CENTRIPETAL WORSHIP
The Evangelical Heart of Lutheran Worship

Copyright © 2007 Augsburg Fortress. All rights reserved. Except for brief quo-
tations in critical articles or reviews, no part of this book may be reproduced
without prior written permission from the publisher. Write to: Permissions,
Augsburg Fortress, Publishers, P. O. Box 1209, Minneapolis, MN 55440-1209.

Editors: Suzanne Burke, Jessica Hillstrom
Cover and interior design: Laurie Ingram
Cover photo: St. Gregory of Nyssa Episcopal Church, San Francisco, California;
© David Sanger

ISBN 978-0-8066-7017-7

Manufactured in the U.S.A.

24   23   22   21   20   19   4   5

Contents

Foreword:
Toward the Center

I was not in town when the gala release of *Evangelical Lutheran Worship* took place at the Augsburg Fortress Bookstore in Philadelphia on October 3, 2006.[1] So, in a few minutes before the bookstore closed on Friday, October 6, I rushed in to purchase a copy. On the way home, at the first red traffic light on Germantown Avenue I opened the book, but rather than finding the front page, my copy began in the back. I thought that perhaps Lutherans had returned to Hebrew! But by the second red traffic light it dawned on me that the cover on my copy of *Evangelical Lutheran Worship* was upside down and backwards. It was too late to return to the bookstore for a new copy, and so I proceeded with my study of the book from back to front.

That means I started with the index of first lines of hymns. Since there aren't any hymns starting with the letter "Z," the first ones I encountered were those starting with words beginning with "Y." "You Servants of God," #825—again toward the back of the book. "You servants of God, your Master proclaim, and publish abroad his wonderful name; the name, all victorious, of Jesus extol; his kingdom is glorious and rules over all!" Yes, Charles Wesley's "Ye servants" was modernized, but my heart was strangely warmed to see that the priestly redactors of *Evangelical Lutheran Worship* had decided that it is okay for Lutherans to sing Wesley's masculine pronouns for Jesus, and, moreover that it is okay to call him "Master," and say that he has a "kingdom." *Evangelical Lutheran Worship* is an inclusive language book, yes, but also it is not exclusive in its inclusivity.

Moving farther up the alphabet (I was still paging backwards), I came upon #502, "The King of love my shepherd is," Henry W. Baker's nineteenth-century christological transposition of Psalm 23. Baker was an Anglican priest and chaired the committee in 1868 that produced the landmark British hymnal *Hymns Ancient and Modern*. Now what I found so reassuring about one of my most favorite hymns is that in *Evangelical Lutheran Worship* the wonderful metaphors that juxtapose the images of the shepherd God in Psalm 23 with Jesus, the good shepherd, were retained. Baker teases us through almost six full stanzas with wonderful images from Psalm 23 transposed into metaphors for Christ and the sacraments. And, you have to sing all six stanzas to get it finally in the last part of the sixth stanza. I appreciate that the editors of *Evangelical Lutheran Worship* did not mess with the metaphors' language.

I once had an argument with the chair of a hymnal committee about the language of hymns. He said that since we don't live in a three-storied universe anymore, all images of "up" and "down" must be changed "to relate to the scientific understandings of a coming generation." What he really meant to say was that the goal was to implode theological and biblical metaphors. When the Gospel of John records that Jesus said to Nicodemus, "You must be born from above" (3:7), Nicodemus didn't get the metaphor and got stuck at the level of gynecology. When we seek to erase the biblical metaphors and images that have embedded themselves into the songs of the church, then singing, and all of worship—to use a wonderful image of Gail Ramshaw—is reduced "to the flattened babble of e-mail."[2] When I seek to worship God, I do not want to receive yet another e-mail, nor do I want to endure another PowerPoint® homily.

Well, I must fast forward. As I paged forward from the hymns, I came to the many pages of service music, ancient and modern, in a multitude of musical and linguistic styles. Marva Dawn says that in worship, "Style is not the issue. What matters is that whatever songs or forms we use keep us aware that God has invited us into worship, that God is present, that God is eminently worthy to receive our praise. . . . The question is whether our worship services immerse us in God's splendor."[3] I am old enough to have lived through a previous incarnation of the "contemporary" versus "traditional" worship wars. I remember more than thirty years ago driving past a church sign that listed two worship services. The 8:00 a.m. service was labeled the "relevant service," and I wondered about what the other one might be! *Evangelical Lutheran Worship* enables congregations to get over the style issue and helps them, instead, to focus on worship that seeks to immerse us into the splendor of God—in many different styles and in the expressions of many cultures both ancient and modern.

My backwards—that is, forward—paging took me through the rich liturgies for occasional services to the front of the book, and what is up front are, of course, liturgies for baptism and word and sacrament. There are ten settings of what Lutherans characteristically refer to as the service of Holy Communion. I would prefer to call them liturgies for word and sacrament, because both word *and* sacrament are one act in the orders of most Christian churches. Check out Frank Senn's comparison on pages 646–647 of his heavy book *Christian Liturgy*. Unfortunately he doesn't include the United Church of Christ (UCC) in his charting of the common shape of liturgy. For my classes in worship leadership with pastors and lay leaders I have pasted electronically the order of the services of word and sacrament in the UCC *Book of Worship* as the sixth listing to demonstrate that, in terminology coined first by Gregory Dix, "the common shape of liturgy in these traditions . . . is more remarkable than the differences."[4]

We all share a common *ordo*, even though in Reformed liturgical traditions the penitential acts are more integral to the services of word and sacrament than in the ten in *Evangelical Lutheran Worship*. We all, with some liturgical and idiosyncratic embellishments, share in a common order of bath, word, meal, and sending. And all of us believe that holy communion or the eucharist or whatever we may wish to call it is normative for each Lord's day. John Calvin insisted on weekly eucharist. However, even though the mass was celebrated, as Professor Wengert writes in chapter 1, with "fearsome regularity" in the sixteenth-century church, folks were accustomed, after the Lateran IV council of 1215, to receiving the bread once a year (p. 15).

When in 1537 Calvin made his proposal for weekly communion to the leadership in Geneva, the Council responded, as many churches still do, with the seven last words song—you know how it goes: "We never did it that way before." Calvin and the Council compromised on communion four times a year, and it got stuck that way for more than four centuries in many Reformed churches until the present time. I am sure that certain Lutheran congregations will find themselves starting Sunday services on page 211 of *Evangelical Lutheran Worship*, that is, with the Service of the Word. The editors apologetically include in the introduction on page 210, "Although a weekly celebration of the Lord's supper is the norm, a service of the word of God is also celebrated regularly or occasionally in many places." Apparently even to Lutherans the seven last words song is familiar!

By the way, Lutherans have it easy. It is so easy to get Martin Luther's imprimatur. We in the Reformed camp, however, don't have just one patron saint to invoke. We first have to decide with whom to toss in the hat. Ulrich Zwingli? Marginal. John Calvin? Thumbs up. And then there is Philip Melanchthon and his pupil, Zacharias Ursinus (an important figure among German Reformed Christians and co-author of the *Heidelberg Catechism*), but by then the line in the sand gets a little wiggly, and each side starts start feeling just a bit proprietary in its hagiology. I wish there were a title for this book other than *Evangelical Lutheran Worship*, for it truly is a book of *common ecumenical* worship. It may even occur to some of the ELCA's ecumenical partners who wish to use this book to buy Wite-Out® and eliminate the "Lutheran" label or otherwise delete it from electronic copies.

My backwards/forward paging through *Evangelical Lutheran Worship* has led us, in the end, to Professor Wengert's thesis about "Centripetal Worship," that "worship is a centripetal force, pulling us in to the center . . . [where] we encounter the Trinity. . . ." He continues, "Our liturgy, with its prayers and proclamation, its sacraments and song, cannot point to itself, much less force us to find that center somewhere else in life, but instead witnesses and draws the worshiping assembly to that very center" (pp. 11, 12). So often I have found that when efforts at liturgical renewal attempt to pull people into the center and to encounter there the living God, they end up being buried in the mazes of ecclesiastical bureaucracy or, worse, simply are treated as inconsequential matters in agendas that push the important issues of justice and witness outside the church and its worship life. Then worship, as Professor Wengert points out, is judged either by "how well we have entertained our guests," or, in my estimation, how convincing an argument we have made for folks to join in justice and witness causes outside the church or to engage in exercises of personal piety both in and outside the church. Or worse, in some churches worship is deemed—and sometimes really is—irrelevant. Maybe that was the unsaid message of that church sign I passed more than 30 years ago. The sending that commissions and energizes Christian vocation originates in the *ordo* of liturgy itself and moves from its center in the Christ who encounters us in word and sacrament to the world in which we live and move and have our being.

Despite the seemingly inevitable actualization of Neil Postman's prediction two decades ago that, even in church, we are being entertained to death,[5] some people, I have discovered, desire to find themselves immersed into the center, to experience there a blessing that comes from beyond themselves, and to be blessed for what happens to them when they exit the church door, in Professor Wengert's borrowed phrase from Thomas Schattauer, where they can "glimpse the world and our neighbor from the 'inside out.'" *Evangelical Lutheran Worship* leads people to the edge of the pool and invites them into the sacred plunge.

Thank you for the privilege of allowing me to do this backward/forward paging of *Evangelical Lutheran Worship* with you, and thereby responding to this proposal for centripetal worship with a loud Reformed "Amen."

F. Russell Mitman

1

An Introduction to
<u>Centripetal</u> Worship[6]

to move on
to move toward a center

It makes a great difference to be married to a pastor. If Martin Luther's theology was affected by being one of the first theologians of the church in a very long time to have been married and to have had children, mine has been similarly challenged and deepened by regular contacts with a working pastor. My personal parish experience may be seventeen years old or older, but in daily conversation with my spouse, Ingrid Wengert, I am reminded of what it means regularly to lead a congregation through worship of God and proclamation of the gospel.

Yet, one of the things from this interaction that has most profoundly affected me did not come as the result of worship at St. Matthew Lutheran Church in Moorestown, New Jersey, where she serves, but arose instead out of our joint experience in a congregation far from home, while we were both on vacation. To be sure, we have no criticism of the congregation or its pastors and have no doubt that they are all eager to serve God faithfully. In fact, I owe the congregation a debt of gratitude, so to speak, because our joint experience of a worship service led me to realize something about worship—all worship—and preaching—all preaching—that I had either taken for granted or, more likely, never really had known. And, had *my* pastor and partner not pointed it out to me as we were driving two hours to the airport, I would still be in the dark.

I wish I could remember her exact words, but the gist of it was simply this: everything that was said in the sermon and much of what happened in the rest of worship that day pointed the hearers and participants away from what was going on in worship, as if nothing of *real* importance for their life of faith was going on there. Taken together, the sermon and the surrounding liturgy functioned with centrifugal force to drive people away from worship of God in that place at that time.

The following comments are not designed to make a bad example of this particular parish. In fact, if, upon reading this, those who now lead worship or who will lead worship simply become more smug in their own ability, then this story will have failed to make its point, because the egregious things that were said and done in worship that Sunday go on in all of our worship spaces. Ever since our first parents looked away from God's promise and toward the eye-pleasing fruit, we have been plagued with this original liturgical sin.

Perhaps some illustrations from that day, however, may help us discover these sins in our own worship leadership. The pastor did preach on the appointed text for the second Sunday after Easter: doubting Thomas. And he did a good job of showing that Thomas was a believing doubter, even as we are. But then he came to the meat of the sermon, or so it seemed. How was he going to apply the story to us? Well, suddenly Thomas became a good example for us to follow, which is probably true if only we could buckle down and do it. But even that was not where the real problem lay. First, the preacher suggested that we pray. That is, *when we got home*, we should find a quiet time and a good place to pray. Then, he suggested that, like Thomas, we should meet with friends. That is, *when we got home*, we should seek out a few trusted mentors and ask for their guidance.

Finally, based upon these two things—perhaps there were more—he suggested that we should expect to meet Jesus in our doubts and faith. That is, *when we got home*, we should look for Jesus in our lives.

Now, please understand! It is not wrong to pray at home, to ask for guidance from friends, in order to see Jesus in our daily life. But we were in church! In a few minutes, one of the pastors would lead us in prayer *in that very space*. The pastor was standing up in the pulpit, a man who was well-liked, approachable and caring—not only that, one who had been called by God through that very congregation to proclaim God's word on Sunday morning *from that very pulpit*! Where else should one go for guidance? Especially when the pastor's words are not his or hers at all but are the very voice of God! Finally, we were also about to celebrate the Lord's supper! We were in *the very place where Christ promises* to show up for all believing doubters with his wounded body and blood given and shed for us all, where he invites us to put our hands in his wounded side, or, to speak more graphically, to put our mouth and tongue on his body and blood.

One can see how far the sermon drove us from the center. And when for the offering song a teen band played and sang unclear lyrics to an unclearly Christian song where the center and focus was the music and the performers, they were, in fact, merely imitating not St. Thomas, but their pastor. Buy the CD so you can learn and listen to the words *at home*. But it could as easily have been a Bach chorale, spoken in perfect German: great for the emotions, perhaps not as hard on the eardrums, but finally pushing us away from worship and into ourselves and our boozy memories of grand chorales gone by.

So the focus of this book is, simply, "Centripetal Worship," because it has to do with the pull into the center. In fact, as Gordon Lathrop once wrote, all Christian worship has to do with the center and the edges—the real center of Christian faith and the edges of human existence.[7] But more about the second point later. For now it is important to consider what it means that Christian worship is a centripetal force, pulling us in to the center, to the one name "given among mortals by which we must be saved" (Acts 4:12), to the one about whom Paul could confess, "May I never boast of anything except the cross of our Lord Jesus Christ" (Gal. 6:14), and who admitted to another worshiping community, "I decided to know nothing among you except Christ, and him crucified" (1 Cor. 2:2). At the center of Christian worship we encounter the Trinity and, even more, Christ crucified and risen again for us. This merciful God stands at the center of our worship. And our liturgy, with its prayers and proclamation, its sacraments and song, cannot point to itself, much less force us to find that center somewhere else in life, but instead witnesses and draws the worshiping assembly to that very center.

Some worship leaders may at this point want quickly to run to Martin Luther's doctrine of vocation and argue that if we are not about the business of equipping people on Sunday to live out their Christian lives during the rest of the week, then we run the risk of turning our liturgy in on itself and making liturgy irrelevant to our daily existence. Yet such an argument, when it arises at this early point in a discussion of worship, masks the hidden assumption that drives all forms of pious religiosity—liberal or conservative—namely, that liturgy is only what we make of it and that the God whom we encounter or, rather, who encounters us in word and sacrament, is powerless to transform our lives in that encounter but waits upon us to act or react. That is, like our preacher described at the outset of this essay, we assume that the real action is elsewhere and that worship itself is powerless to do anything for us or to us, for that one hour on Sunday let alone for the rest of the week.

Centripetal worship in the history of the church

The notion of such centripetal Christian worship is not new. In fact, not simply the words of the Hebrew scriptures but the actions it describes witness to this centripetal force. The portable altar with the *kabod YHWH* (glory of the Lord) that fills the center of the Tent of Meeting and leads the people is not simply a sweet story but a central image for the true actions of God in worship. Similarly, in the New Testament, the eschatological worship described in Revelation places God and the Lamb in the center of the city that needs no temple. True Christian worship does not compete with or undermine either vision. Indeed, one would not be so far off the mark to say that these earliest and latest descriptions of worship in the Bible are exactly the same and, thus, all worship in between points us both to the beginning and the end. We worship, by faith alone, as members of both Israel and the New Israel. That is, God still puts the same center at the heart of our gathering—the same portable altar and the same center in the open-gated city of Paradise.

Others know far more about the contours of biblical worship than this author, so that it would be foolish to pretend that one could in a single paragraph seize the brass ring for the biblical interpretation of worship. Much less do I have the breadth of knowledge to provide a convincing description of the history of Christian worship. However, given what I do know about Martin Luther and the Reformation, the reader will forgive me for jumping ahead to the sixteenth century, not because it is the be-all and end-all of Christian worship, but simply because it is what I have studied the most.[8]

There have been many attempts to describe church life on the eve of the Reformation. Yet, it would seem to me that one word, namely, the antonym of the title of this book, may suffice: *centrifugal* worship. Everything pulled people away from the Sunday assembly and into themselves and the work that they could do for the salvation of their souls. One fact, gleaned from the splendid article by Helmar Junghans on Luther's reform of worship, may suffice as introduction to this state of affairs.[9] Consider the city of Wittenberg in 1519. To be sure, every Sunday the faithful could gather in the city church of St. Mary's and witness from a distance the Lord's supper and hear preaching. Down the street at the Castle Church, however, priests would in the course of that year celebrate more than 6,000 private masses for the souls of deceased members of the princely family that ruled electoral Saxony. At St. Mary's, too, as well as at the churches of the town's monastic institutions, private masses were held. But that is not all. In many of the larger cities in the Holy Roman Empire of the German Nation there was, to be sure, preaching. However, with the obvious exception of Wittenberg, where Luther was already proclaiming a different message, the point of such preaching would have often been to urge people to take part in the sacrament of penance. That is, the sermon would have pointed them away from the worship in that place and not only to an act of the church that took place outside of worship but also, given the regnant theology of that day, to themselves and their powers. For, as the late-medieval theologian Gabriel Biel often reminded his readers, "To those who do what is in them, God will not deny grace."[10]

If Martin Luther's own reminiscences are accurate, such preaching also depicted Christ not as welcoming savior but as perfect example or coming judge. To protect oneself from his wrath, the believer was pointed away from him and toward his mother, who on the Last Day would bare her breasts to her angry son and pray to him for the poor souls huddling under her robes. "How can you deny the request of the one who nursed you?" she would ask. But even Mary's robe, far from simply pointing the way into God's mercy, consisted instead, according to at least one late-medieval catechism, of the good works of believers.[11]

The Lord's supper, celebrated with fearsome regularity, did not draw people together toward God's merciful presence but rather, in many ways, away from one another and from God. First, literal and figurative high fences prevented participation. The rood screen not only separated spiritual and secular people but also prevented people from seeing and hearing what was going on. The language prevented people from hearing God's promises in two ways: by being in Latin and by having the central words of Christ's promise whispered, so that even the attendants at the altar could not hear them. The division of the sacrament, which forbade the laity from receiving both bread and wine, also contributed to a certain alienation. Christ's presence, confirmed by the Lateran IV council in 1215, also pushed people away from the meal, because worthy eating and drinking of transubstantiated bread and wine required thorough confession of all one's sins before one could encounter Christ. The requirement to receive the supper once a year meant that the vast majority of people did just that and no more. Thus, members of the Roman Oratory of Divine Love, a sixteenth-century renewal movement in Italy, who promised to attend mass daily and receive the sacrament monthly, were considered unusually pious.[12]

We all have heard tales of the selling of indulgences. The procession of the chief indulgence preacher, accompanied by the papal coat-of-arms and the leaders of the city, wended its way from the city gates to the largest church in town, while the bells and organs in all the churches sounded. The preaching, of course, drove people not toward God and their neighbor but away from them and to the sacrament of penance, that is, into their pocketbooks and toward the money chest—indeed toward Rome and purgatory. Of course, before we smile politely at the quaint ways in which Christians lost track of the center, let us reflect upon whether we do the same. We fill our worship with announcements and pleas for giving; we imply that paying off a debt to a Lutheran insurance agency has spiritual *gravitas*; or we assume that what finally matters is how well we have entertained our guests.

Into this welter of centrifugal worship practices Luther spoke a reforming word. Here, before we go into any detail, we must consider where Luther began or, more to the point, where he did not begin. This consideration, indeed, will help us view later Lutheran worship books, especially *Evangelical Lutheran Worship*, from an evangelical perspective. Luther did not begin his reform of worship with a search for rules. Already the New Testament helps us, if we recall that, despite the overwhelming centrality of worship for the early Christians, no liturgical rulebook appears in the New Testament canon. Even the one later ancient text that is sometimes cited as a rulebook, the Didache, is, as my colleague Dirk Lange has shown, just the opposite.[13] Moreover, in Psalm 137 the Hebrew scriptures help us even more by posing the central liturgical question of the Exile to us: "How can we sing the LORD's song in a foreign land?" And the foreign land in which our New Testament stood was not just the Greek-speaking world but a world in which God's Son was raised from the dead, the new world of Easter. Even for a latecomer like the author of Hebrews, who admits to knowing everything secondhand, no more sacrifice is required because Christ is sacrificed *ephapax*, "once for all." No wonder that during the Third Reich, Dietrich Bonhoeffer's secret seminary, in the face of the foreign land in which they lived and died, had inscribed on its altar that same Greek word.

In the face of all our attempts to discover the rules for correct worship, we can only confess with Luther that Christian worship, true worship, is not about us and our rules but about God in Christ, who is the end of the law. As Dirk Lange has observed, Luther thinks there is but one "law" for the church's mass, Jesus Christ himself![14] It is not about repristinating or remembering a particularly beloved past, not about our sacrificing, and certainly not about moral pep talks. At the center of Christian worship is the promise of Christ crucified and risen again; at the center is the voice from heaven, the baptism of the beloved Son, and the heavenly, hovering Dove; at the center is the body and blood of Christ for us.

Here, finally, we discover where we might begin to appreciate one of the accomplishments of *Evangelical Lutheran Worship*—not in the specifics of Luther's suggestions for a reform of worship, but in the center. There have been enough complaints and compliments of *Evangelical Lutheran Worship* and, for that matter, of *Lutheran Book of Worship* to realize that the search for rules goes on. Why was my favorite hymn not included? Here is a list of my least favorite that should not have been included. Thank you—or curse you—for following inclusive language rules! Why were you not more—or less—

inclusive? How can you call yourselves Lutheran? Why bother calling ourselves Lutheran? Why aren't there more rules? Why aren't there fewer? Why aren't they more ecumenical? Why aren't they less?

For those who worked throughout the heat of the day on this new worship resource and for those who use it, I have good news! Christian worship, true worship, is not about this remarkable achievement in *Evangelical Lutheran Worship*. It is about God. In Christian worship, true worship, God acts. In baptism, the heavens are ripped open, the voice sounds, the Dove hovers, and the beloved Son stands dripping wet in the Jordan! In the supper, the Christ who humbled himself and came among us as a servant, obedient unto death, comes in the last place you or I would reasonably look, with bread and wine for forgiveness, life, and salvation wrapped like a towel around his waist, washing our mouths and souls. And in the word we hear not the voice of the preacher but the very voice of God, the real auditory presence of the one who approaches all who are crippled by sin, and says, "Take heart, your sins are forgiven." Viewed in that light, one can only give thanks that this current work witnesses to and serves that center.

Centripetal worship in this volume

In his book *The Pastor: A Spirituality* Gordon Lathrop reflects on the pastor's preparation for leading worship with these words.

> But, besides this lifelong task, an actual, weekly rehearsal is also a good idea. To stand in the place of the assembly—together with the other communal leaders or, if necessary, alone—to imagine the flow of the event, to consider where each person is to be and whether the door will be open to yet others, to try on the words and the music in the space, … to savor and treasure the importance of assembly, to learn it by heart—this is also a spiritual practice.[15]

These words summarize the major themes in this book. This chapter and the next one will help the readers "savor and treasure the importance of assembly" by learning what is at its heart. Melinda Quivik's contribution will lead readers "to consider where each person is to be." Dirk Lange's reflections on evangelism lead to a consideration of "whether the door will be open to yet others." And Mark Mummert will aid us in "trying on the words and the music." As we learn these things by heart, we will find ourselves swept up, by the power of the Holy Spirit, into the very center of worship, Jesus Christ, crucified and risen for us.

Sunflowers grow centripetally, with the youngest part of the flower in the center. May all of our worship resources, but especially *Evangelical Lutheran Worship* and the church's use of it, become such a sunflower. And may a thousand flowers bloom.

For reflection and discussion

1. What is centripetal worship?
2. Have you ever experienced its opposite? What was it like?
3. Martin Luther's day provided some notorious examples of the opposite of centripetal worship (see pp. 13–15). How do we sometimes do the same?
4. What happens when people reduce Christian worship to following rules? What is the proper role of rules in Christian worship?

2
Martin Luther's Witness to the Center of Worship

It is no accident that the essays in a book celebrating *Evangelical Lutheran Worship* come from teachers at the Lutheran Theological Seminary at Philadelphia, the one seminary in the Evangelical Lutheran Church in America and its predecessors that can rightfully claim to have contributed in significant ways to four of the last five major worship books in North American Lutheranism: *The Common Service Book* of the nineteenth century, *The Lutheran Hymnal* of the Lutheran Church—Missouri Synod (through the inclusion of the Common Service), *Service Book and Hymnal*, and, now, *Evangelical Lutheran Worship*. In each case, the intention has been to witness to the center in the particular times for which these books were produced.

In this intention, these books and their many collaborators stand in a direct line to the remarkable liturgical work of Martin Luther. After all, what do we have in Luther's Latin and German orders for holy communion (the *Formula Missae* and the *Deutsche Messe*), or in his services for absolution, baptism, marriage, or in his hymns and those of his contemporaries? We have not rules but a witness to the center. No wonder that, when Lucas Cranach, the Saxon court painter who lived in Wittenberg, came to paint the central altar in that city, he depicted Luther in Wittenberg's pulpit, pointing, like John the Baptist, to the cross, on which hangs the Lamb of God who takes away the sin of the world. Moreover, in the scene of the Lord's supper directly above Luther, Cranach painted one of the twelve apostles to look like Luther as he appeared in 1521, when for the first time in Wittenberg the laity received the cup. And, indeed, Luther is turning to offer the chalice to a *layman* in sixteenth-century dress.

No wonder that Luther prefaces his baptismal liturgy with the invitation for others to do better. If we use his famous "Flood Prayer" (part of the baptismal service in both *Lutheran Book of Worship* and *Evangelical Lutheran Worship*) just because he wrote it or just because it is in the book, then we are merely following the rules and are turning baptism into a faithless rite, but if it expresses our own deepest faith and the fervent prayers of our faith community, then splash around in it and let everyone get soaked with Luther's witness.

Luther's appeal for centripetal worship did not simply come in his writings reforming various parts of the liturgy from 1523 and later but may be seen already in 1520, in his famous *On the Babylonian Captivity of the Church*.[16] The title alone points out how dangerous it is to move away from the center in the sacraments and, thus, in the worship life of Luther's church. The church has been *carried away* into captivity by the misuse of the sacraments and must now be brought back to the center. For Luther, that center is nothing other than the ordinances and unconditional promises of God. In the supper, God ordained bread *and* wine; Christ's promise to show up does not depend upon Aristotelian physics (that is, the Roman doctrine of transubstantiation);[17] and Christ's testament overturns human notions of sacrifice. In baptism, no promise—not even a monastic vow—trumps God's promise. When Luther turns back to the center, he discovers the supper, baptism, and baptism's companion, the daily forgiveness of sin—each a setting for the word. Everything must serve the center. Thus, because confirmation had simply become a rite reserved for bishops with no connection to baptism in those days, ordination an opportunity to set people apart to say private masses for the dead, and last rites a pretense to terrify the dying and their loved ones, they could no longer be counted as sacraments.[18] Marriage, of which Luther approved, served another center altogether—God's work in creation. Thus, it was no more a Christian sacrament than breathing or building a house or governing a country. As he later makes clear in his preface to the revised marriage service, the church does not perform marriages; it rather pronounces God's blessing upon an already married couple.[19]

In the midst of this rediscovery of centripetal worship, Luther also provided certain insights into the nature of liturgy and worship that may help us today as well. In Wittenberg, there was worship for all kinds of people. That worship was not "new" but drank deeply from the rich variety of Christian worship throughout the ages. It respected the incarnational nature of the language we use to worship God. And, most importantly, it eliminated all language of sacrifice in order to make clear that what happens in worship is not what we do for God but what God says and does to us.

Worship for all kinds

Evangelical Lutheran Worship, with its countless ways to order worship within the one *ordo* of word, sacraments, prayer, and praise is not doing something new but instead following the lead of Martin Luther. According to the work of Helmar Junghans, from the mid-1520s onward, the opportunities for worship in Wittenberg were quite diverse.[20] On Sundays alone, three very different worship services served very different parts of the highly diverse Wittenberg congregation. Early in the morning, Matins, with preaching on the appointed epistle lesson, especially served the servants and workers in the burgher and farm households, whose daily chores made it much more difficult for them to worship later. Then came the main service, always a celebration of the Lord's supper with preaching on the appointed gospel, for the vast majority of Wittenberg's citizens. For the most part, this worship was done in German, but not always. The Latin service, which was the *lingua franca* of the time, served the intelligentsia, but in particular the foreign students, of whom there were often hundreds in Wittenberg. Incidentally, as a further accommodation to non-German speakers, Philip Melanchthon gave Latin explanations of the gospel text at 7 a.m. on Sunday mornings, first in his home but later, when the crowds of students grew too large, in a university lecture hall.

In the evening, Vespers was held where a variety of texts from the Hebrew Scriptures or the New Testament were preached upon. Four times a year, at the Embers (that is, around Ash Wednesday, Pentecost, Holy Cross Day [September 14], and St. Andrew's Day [November 30]), a series of sermons were held on Sunday afternoons and throughout the week that were designed especially for children and families and based upon the "catechism" of the Ten Commandments, Apostles' Creed, Lord's Prayer, baptism, and the Lord's supper. During Holy Week and Easter, services were held daily, during which time the Lord's supper, absolution, and, of course, Christ's death and resurrection would be explained for the simple folk. On Wednesdays and Saturdays, Vespers were dedicated to preaching through the gospels of Matthew and John respectively, in what might be considered the sixteenth-century equivalent of Bible studies, where the center was not self-centered knowledge and piety of the teacher but the proclamation of God's grace and the praise of God's name. Among the university students there were also opportunities for services in Latin that used the wide variety of ancient and more recent Latin hymns and sequences.

In some ways, it is sad that modern Lutherans have had to relearn from the current culture ways to accommodate "the other" in worship, when Luther and his Wittenbergers, in their own context, had been doing the same thing ages ago—not to sell out God's word to the culture but rather to accommodate the word to the variety of folks who needed to hear it. Paraphrasing Paul, Luther might as well be saying, "To the Bauer [peasant], I became a Bauer; to the Latin student, a Latin student; to the burgher, a burgher"—not simply to go with the times but to witness to the center. Like its predecessors, *Evangelical Lutheran Worship* strives to do this, too, with its remarkable variety of hymns and settings of the liturgy.

Here, however, a word must be said about the edges of Christian worship. Worship for Luther also involved collecting for the poor. The community chest often stood in the city churches of the Reformation and provided money for the pastor and the school-master, no-interest loans for working poor, and direct aid for the aged, infirm, and refugees. In the rare times that note-takers of Luther's sermons did not hear the "Amen" and went on to record the parish announcements and prayers, we discover that Luther sometimes urged, from the pulpit, that payments to that chest be made. "I have made my contribution," he once said, "Why haven't more of you made yours?"[21] Here, finally, in the Christian concern for those on the margins, the Wittenberg congregation became an answer to Luther's plea already in the 95 Theses *not* to spend money on indulgences but to spend it on the poor. Of course, to encourage such activity in the congregation was not to lose sight of the center at all but rather to realize that "When I was naked, you clothed me; hungry, you fed me...." Thus, Luther upbraids his congregation in a Christmas sermon. "You say, 'If I had been there, I would have helped Mary.' Sure, you can say that now because you know who her child was. Why do you not help the poor, who are Christ in your midst?"[22] Thus, at the fringes, we encounter the center. And, at the center, the fringes. The "new" sending in *Evangelical Lutheran Worship*, "Go in peace. Remember the poor" should perhaps, if our giving were done in this spirit, be moved to the offering where we could say, paraphrasing Paul in Galatians, "We begin in peace; we have remembered the poor!" (2:10). Or perhaps, better still, as the second-century Christian teacher, Justin Martyr, indicates was done in his day, we could put the offering at the end of the service and send the people out past the collection boxes by saying, "Go in peace! Remember the poor!"

Such a movement from the center to the fringes puts the lie to all forms of centrifugal worship, which sends people "out" by sending them away from Christ and into themselves. Then worship becomes an excuse for practicing personal piety, giving some sop for the poor to soothe the conscience, or simply patting them on the head and saying, "Be of good cheer" or "Hate the sin; love the sinner" or "God helps those who help themselves." Only from the center, from Christ and his wounded hands and feet can we, wounded by sin, be transformed to run on broken feet to the fringes and offer our wounded hands. Only then, borrowing a phrase from Thomas Schattauer, can we glimpse the world and our neighbor from the "inside out."[23]

Witness from all times

Althought Mark Mummert will discuss hymnody more extensively in the next chapter, this is the place to say a word about hymns. When it comes to hymnody, Luther's example is precisely the one followed in *Evangelical Lutheran Worship*—to an even greater extent than in its immediate predecessor. When Luther went to form German hymnody for his congregation, he did not—despite the popular legend—ever go to bars. Instead, he tapped the inexhaustible, Spirit-led Christians of 1,500 years before him, nay, rather, of 2,500 years before him. Using the Pauline line about "psalms, hymns, and spiritual songs" (Col. 3:16), Luther understood the first term to designate the Hebrew Psalter, the second the canticles of the New Testament, and the third the hymns of all Christians since.[24] Thus, we sing Ambrose today because Luther realized that that ancient bishop's hymns drew the Wittenberg congregation into the center, toward the word of God. For the same reason, we sing Hildegard of Bingen, Juliana of Norwich, or Elizabeth Cruciger, to say nothing of Philip Nicolai or Charles Wesley.

Consider Elizabeth Cruciger, an escaped nun from a noble family (von Meseritz). She later married Caspar Cruciger, who became Luther's colleague at the University of Wittenberg in the 1530s. In 1524, as Luther and others were compiling the first evangelical hymnbook, they included her amazing hymn, "The only Son from heaven." Later, when grumpy Lutherans objected that one should not sing the words of a woman in church, because Paul had insisted they be silent (some hymnals even attributed her poem to a man), other Lutherans happily responded with the prophet Joel's words that in the last days, sons *and daughters* would prophesy (2:28).[25] Thus, at least in Germany where her hymn is often sung in the time after Epiphany, the church has ordained that a woman lead prayers and proclamation in the Christian assembly since 1524. The last stanza of her hymn reads "Slay us with your goodness; enlighten us through grace. Bring to the old such sickness, that we new life embrace."[26]

Martin Luther also created new hymns and wrote new music—sometimes based upon old tunes and sometimes not. He thereby unleashed a creative spirit in Lutheranism and, indeed, in the whole church that continues to this day. Words and music for Luther serve one purpose and one purpose only: to proclaim the Word made flesh. Thereby, Luther's own hymnody supplies an amazing variety of pictures, writing new songs and hymns and rewriting old psalms and canticles. Without robbing ourselves of his picturesque language—where God may be a loving Father watching over our every need or Lord Sabaoth obscured by billowing smoke, where Christ can be the dearest child for our hearts or a knight in shining armor battling sin, death, and the devil, and where the Holy Spirit can be creator, comforter, or sweet lover—we follow in his footsteps when we discover old and new ways, from all corners of the church, for praising the Trinity, drawing people in toward the center. *Evangelical Lutheran Worship* does this eloquently.

Bringing order out of chaos: incarnational language

Word, table, bath, prayer.[27] They are not our actions for God but God's for us. As *Evangelical Lutheran Worship* itself proclaims, "The Holy Spirit gathers the people of God around Jesus Christ present in the word of God and the sacraments, so that the Spirit may in turn send them into the world to continue the ingathering mission of God's reign" (*Evangelical Lutheran Worship*, p. 6). Through these actions, our worship takes an incarnational form, one that is neither speculative nor spiritualized.

Consider how God's speaking, feeding, and gathering worked in the Reformation. In my research on the so-called Osiandrian controversy, a dispute among Lutherans shortly after Luther's death over the nature of our salvation in Christ, I have read over seventy tracts that Lutherans wrote in that fight. The gist of the dispute boiled down to this: What makes us righteous before God? The imputed righteousness of Christ crucified (the Lutheran position) or the perfect, infused righteousness of his divine nature (Andreas Osiander's position)? Most of this literature had not been read over the last 450 years, and for good reason. But every once in a while, some voice breaks through time, language, and culture, and speaks to us directly.

What if you were Joachim Mörlin, who had just lost his position as pastor because of his dogged refusal to bow to his prince's wishes and support Osiander? What if you now lived in exile, hundreds of miles from your dear flock and family, a flock from which more than 400 women and children marched to the princely castle in the freezing cold to beg the return of their pastor and, when they were refused an audience, sang in protest three of Luther's lament hymns before they left. Suppose your enemy, as he was about to drive you out of the country, accused you of having said in a sermon that you did not know who God was. Would you have the courage to say what Mörlin both said from his pulpit before he was driven out of town and wrote in an account of that sermon two years later while in exile?

Like Luther, he knew where the heart of worship lay. His opponent, I venture to say, did not.

> And to this extent I confess now just as I also confessed then, that I did not only preach that we do not *know* what God is *in God's essence*—let alone try to discuss and talk about it (as Gregory of Nazianzus, Augustine, Ambrose and Hilary[28] also write)—but I said even more. The Scripture also talks very little about who God is in God's very self, namely, God the Father, Son and Holy Spirit. Instead, it talks for the most part about what God is for us: namely God is merciful, who lets our misery abate and moves us gently, who suffers with us and takes upon himself such misery. Thus, I defend myself from raving speculators as from the devil, those who want to interpret absolutely words with relational meanings that refer to specific contexts. Thus, for them, the righteousness of God becomes that by which God is righteous in God's very being. Watch out! Or, flee to the Bible, which shows our dear God wearing baby shoes [*Kinderschuhen*] and draws God out of that heavenly essence (within which God can never be understood in this life) to be among us, in that God speaks, has eyes, ears, hands, feet, which God actually does not have. Not, I say, in God's divine essence, as God is in God's very self from all eternity, but instead as God came into the world and walked among us. Oh my! Look at how John makes himself happy and is filled with joy about this and says, "We have also seen the glory of the only begotten Son." Where is that, dear John, where is that? "He is lying in a manger, has hands and feet, body and soul," that is, "The Word became flesh."[29]

Now, if Joachim Mörlin, one of the first people ever to be called (in a positive sense) a gnesio-Lutheran (genuine Lutheran), gets the point about language and the center, how can we do less? Or perhaps, most positively said, this point is one of many things that *Evangelical*

Lutheran Worship does get, with little speculation about God in God's self and, instead, a Johannine happiness and joy in giving God hands, feet, body, and soul. And here I do not primarily mean to praise the inclusive language—that is finally an adiaphoron[30] and must bow low to pastoral discretion and intelligence, something that *Evangelical Lutheran Worship* allows for through its variety of worship forms, music, and hymnody. What I mean here is what Mörlin means—contenting ourselves with a riot of metaphors, clothing God in any and all language, always with an eye toward John 1:14. If Ambrose can get away with referring to Christ in an Advent hymn as a kind of Atlas—and we still sing his hymn fifteen centuries later—then we can relish and seek out all the best poets on earth to bring us new and startling ways to introduce the scandal of the gospel—"The Word became flesh!"[31]

No more sacrifice

Of course, at the heart of Luther's worship revolution, to which we are heirs in *Evangelical Lutheran Worship*, is the elimination of the sacrifice of the mass. Now here we need to proceed with caution and note carefully what Luther did and did not do. Late-medieval liturgical piety had filled the canon of the mass with prayers to the saints and offerings up of an unbloodied sacrifice to the Father for the sins of those gathered or those in whose memory the mass had been bought. Luther did not eliminate those prayers because he was against praying and proclaiming in the same breath but because such prayers took people away from the center. They made the priest and the praying community the center and God the helpless hospital chaplain, running back and forth from one demanding patient to the next with a frantic presence and words. *Ephapax* (once for all) means no more sacrifices. Christ's grace is the center; God's love is the heart; the Holy Spirit's communion is the promise.

In fact, Luther did not in his German service, or, for that matter, in his Latin service, eliminate the eucharistic prayer; he merely replaced the medieval language of a priest offering a sacrifice to God with the much older language of God sacrificing for us, that is, with the Lord's Prayer, which he placed *before*, not after, the words of institution. Moreover, Luther set the words of institution to the gospel tone. That is, in his order of worship he assigned that text to be sung to the same chant tone used for singing the gospel of the day. He also mixed in praise for God's presence in the Sanctus (Holy, holy, holy) and the Agnus Dei (Lamb of God).[32] Then, he eliminated all of the imploring of the late-medieval canon, letting the all-encompassing petitions of the Lord's Prayer suffice.

But Luther also did not intend the words of institution to become a kind of magic formula recited as a way of making Christ show up. The liturgical practice of some Lutherans in later centuries may actually have left that impression by reciting words mindlessly (often turned away from the congregation) and with little sense of thanksgiving. At the same time, every time we do use eucharistic prayers to grace Christ's promise in the supper, we dare not let them once again obscure that promise so that we may busily start sacrificing all over again. The offering prayer, in particular, has rightly become in *Evangelical Lutheran Worship* an option and not a requirement, just to show that we are free of all forms of sacrifice, even "sacrificial" giving. Christ shows up for us not because we say certain words or prayers or give money; we say those words and prayers to proclaim Christ's very promise ("Here I am for you") and to give thanks.

In fact, in the 1540s when Wittenberg's theologians were asked to consider when, exactly, Christ was present with the bread and wine, its two chief reformers gave very different but equally helpful answers.[33] For Melanchthon, who with Martin Bucer and others feared bread worship, Christ should never get "trapped" in the bread. For Luther, who worried that Christ might be more absent than present in his meal, Christ is there from the time the elements reach the table until the final blessing. No wonder he placed the elevation (until it was eliminated in the late 1530s) at the singing of the Sanctus. Even after the blessing, he insisted that the elements be treated as special and not like yesterday's leftovers. Yet, for both theologians, the point is to witness to the center—Christ's promised presence, here tied to the actual use of the elements in the assembly.

What a useful, Lutheran book *Evangelical Lutheran Worship* is, that allows us both to utter Christian prayers of thanksgiving, not sacrificial ones, as the setting for the proclamation of Christ's promise to be present and, once again, to sing those words as gospel for the whole world to hear. Would that our children would start running around the house after worship, humming, "Our Lord Jesus Christ in the night in which he was betrayed" along with the Gloria in excelsis (Glory to God), the Sanctus, and the Agnus Dei—all spiritual songs, by the way, that celebrate Christ's presence for us in this meal, that point us to the center.

It can happen. When I was a parish pastor in Wisconsin, the worship committee decided to return to a familiar setting of the liturgy because a member, an oil hauler by occupation, complained that the new music was too hard for him to sing in his truck as he worked. My spouse, pastor in Moorestown, New Jersey, told me much more recently of a little boy who was about to join our congregation. "I never before got up on Sunday morning eager to come to worship," his mother explained. "And my son loves to walk around the house singing a song about this feast." May we all learn such excitement, as worship draws us and all kinds of people out of ourselves into the center, where, with the whole church of all ages, we praise and feed on our incarnate Savior and Lord!

For reflection and discussion

1. How would you describe Luther's overall claim to centripetal worship?
2. The author describes four different contributions that Luther made to worship and shows how *Evangelical Lutheran Worship* reflects the same concerns. How is your worship for "all kinds" and how might your concern for the people on the fringes increase?
3. How does your worship take resources from the entire church and its history and how might this process improve?
4. How is the language of worship "incarnational" and, thus, reflective of the wide variety of human expression and praise?
5. In what ways do we still confuse our sacrifice and works for true Christian worship, where God provides avenues for grace and mercy to us, especially coming to us with Christ's body and blood in the bread and wine?

3
Musical Power:
Broken to the Center

A small group of young men and women gathered to pray evening prayer. This group formed an academy dedicated to the theological education of youth and had been gathering daily for two weeks to pray the office of evening prayer using a variety of leadership and ceremony. On this particular evening, they were keeping the annual commemoration of Johann Sebastian Bach (July 28). To everyone's great joy, they honored the commemoration with music composed by the great cantor of the church, sung and played with great skill and delight by the academy scholars. They came expecting life-giving music and the opportunity to give thanks to God for the gift of music, and particularly J. S. Bach. They did not come, however, expecting the word of God to surprise them.

By the joyous movement of the Holy Spirit, one of the readings for the day assigned by the daily lectionary was a story about Elisha. The pericope for the day began soon after the lifting of Elijah by a whirlwind into heaven (2 Kings 2:1-18), and the passing of the mantle of leadership to Elisha, who was able to work miracles (2 Kings 2:19-25). At that time, a conflict was rising between King Mesha of Moab and

King Jehoram of Israel in Samaria, and several kings joined together, with their armies, to set out for battle. By the seventh day of their journey the water for all in the army, and the animals, had run out (2 Kings 3:1-8).

> Then the king of Israel said. "Alas! The LORD has summoned us, three kings, only to be handed over to Moab." But Jehoshaphat [the king of Judah] said, "Is there no prophet of the LORD here, through whom we may inquire of the LORD?" Then one of the servants of the king of Israel answered, "Elisha son of Shaphat, who used to pour water on the hands of Elijah, is here." Jehoshaphat said, "The word of the LORD is with him." So the king of Israel and Jehoshaphat and the king of Edom went down to him. Elisha said to the king of Israel, "What have I to do with you? Go to your father's prophets or to your mother's." But the king of Israel said to him, "No; it is the LORD who has summoned us, three kings, only to be handed over to Moab." Elisha said, "As the LORD of hosts lives, whom I serve, were it not that I have regard for King Jehoshaphat of Judah, I would give you neither a look nor a glance. *But get me a musician.*" *And then, while the musician was playing, the power of the LORD came on him.* And he said, "Thus says the LORD, 'I will make this wadi full of pools.' For thus says the LORD, 'You shall see neither wind nor rain, but the wadi shall be filled with water, so that you shall drink, you, your cattle and your animals'" (2 Kings 3: 9-17, emphasis added).

"Get me a musician," Elisha finally instructed, coming to the end of his patience and giving in to their persistence. The musician arrived, played music, and the power of God came to Elisha. What did she play? Did she sing?[34] Regardless, by this miracle of music joined to the power of God, water was restored. Curiously, the story of this miracle does not report that anyone reacted to the event with amazement or wonder! It is as if Elisha's request for a musician was a usual occurrence, not extraordinary, almost expected. No one in the text of the story seems surprised that Elisha would call for the musician, or more importantly, that the music the musician played would be used to invoke the very power of God.

The academy scholars that July evening, however, were very surprised! First, the intersection of the commemoration of Bach and this reading of scripture delighted and amazed them. (No doubt the Spirit works even and especially through the church's calendar of readings.) But also, the scripture reading and the annual commemoration invited them to consider the power of God through music, a power that surprises us—even though it should not. In that liturgy of evening prayer, they were welcomed to a celebration of music as a powerful gift of God, able to invoke God's strength and might to create water where there was no water.

The fact that scripture attributes power to music should not surprise us at all. Christians have come to know God through the scriptures as a God whose audible self creates something out of nothing. God speaks, and it is so. "God *said*, 'Let there be light'" (Gen. 1:3). This sound, which creates light, heavens, waters, and human beings, is the audible word of God. Music participates in this great acoustic wave of divine, audible creativity. Furthermore, when God speaks and acts by sound, humans are created and compelled to respond with sound—sounds of proclamation and rejoicing—announcing through music what God's power has done.

Elisha knew of musical power because his ancestors sang songs full of this power, and their song, given to them by God, was full of the word of God. Elisha knew what Moses and Miriam knew when they found themselves on the other side of the sea (Exod. 15); Elisha knew what David and Solomon and the Levitical priests knew as they assembled the faithful to praise and worship (1 Chron. 6); Elisha knew what Mary, and Zechariah, and Simeon knew when they sang around the Word becoming flesh (Luke 1–2); Elisha knew what Paul knew in prison (Acts 16:25) and what John knew in his revelation (Rev. 4–5). Music invokes the power of God to create something out of nothing: water where there was no water, praise where there was only fear of Pharaoh and a merciful escape, proclamation of God's grace and mercy after ancient promises were fulfilled, and a revelation of future restoration after destruction when all the earth sings "Holy, holy, holy." The biblical witness assumes musical power, a power flowing from the power of the triune God, a power to change, gather, praise, proclaim, and propel into action. Music is a sign of God at work in the world. The conviction that the triune God revealed in the scriptures is a God who creates, sustains, and enlivens by audible means is, indeed, a sound theology.

Most of us encounter the power of music in our lives on a daily basis. Upon hearing a song from our past, we are instantly led to recall another time and place; music conjures memory. In a medical office, as we wait to see the doctor, music in the reception room soothes our pulse and eases our anxiety. At the gym, music thumps and beats to propel our workout. Music evokes or propels a physical response from us. Certain music can bring tears or laughter depending on the timbre, harmony, rhythm, and the associations we have with those musical variables. Music manipulates emotion. The songs sung by freedom marchers or striking workers can unite people to join the cause. Music gathers an assembly in purpose.

Much work has been done of late to study the science of musical power. The *New York Times* reported about a hospital where a harpist strolls about the cardiac post-anesthesia care unit two hours a day. The harpist is part of a test to measure the effects of music on the healing process. During the test, recovery room monitors track changes in patients' vital signs every fifteen minutes while she plays, and for an hour before and after. Interestingly, the harpist tries not to play anything recognizable, in order to minimize unwanted emotional responses. The music is chosen specifically to regulate the heart beat, to calm the breathing, such that patients coming out of anesthesia, with tubes protruding from every point in their bodies, can relax into the care that the unit needs to give.[35]

In his book *This Is Your Brain on Music* Dr. Daniel J. Levitin used neuroscience to analyze the elements of music—pitch, rhythm, tempo, timbre, harmony, and melody—to uncover the force they have in our lives. For instance, Levitin discovered that given the same musical composition, the brain has a different chemical reaction whether we hear that music through a recording or hear it in a live performance.[36] Levitin's study also proves that music triggers the reward centers of the brain by releasing dopamine from the nucleus accumbus and ventral tegmental area, causing us instantly to remember and recognize music and engage our long-term memory.[37] As Levitin and other musical scientists help us discover the science behind God's gift of music, we are moved again to listen in awe and wonder.

We also know stories of musical power used in dangerous and problematic ways. Consider the story of composer Hugo Distler, who took his own life at age 34, most assuredly because he was aware of how his own composition was used by the Nazis to celebrate their devious schemes. Music is not partial; it will, like a sponge, take on the context and create associations with its surroundings with such vigor that it is hard for us to separate the context from the music itself. This association poses a deep challenge for us today. Musical power, when in the hands and mouths of humans, can be used for sinful purposes. To be sure, the music is, in and of itself, not evil; the evil lies in us when we manipulate music for our own lusts of power and control.

These truths concerning musical power then lead Christians to ask important questions: What do we do with this musical power? How can Christians, when they gather, use musical power in appropriate ways? Are there dangers with musical power?

Christians have addressed these questions of musical power throughout the ages in a number of ways. Of the great theologians of the church, Augustine, bishop of Hippo in North Africa, was keenly aware of both the gifts and challenges of music in Christian life. He knew of music's ability, when joined to the word of God, to make that word live in both the singer and the hearer in a way that no other medium could fully replicate. But he also knew that music could also divert the singer and the hearer away from the word, because of the emotional and physical power of the music. For this reason, Augustine was somewhat restrictive when counseling the use of music in the Christian communities of his day. On the other hand, his teacher Ambrose, bishop of Milan, found music to be the primary way for the trinitarian faith to be taught to the people. Ambrose trusted the power of music and felt compelled to sing with abandon against the heresies of his time.

Martin Luther also trusted music to be a God-given vehicle for the word of God and was less conflicted about music in the life and worship of Christians. Luther insisted that music was one of God's greatest gifts to humanity. In our time, we easily imagine that music is *our* gift to God—we make our "musical offering," we craft our worship to be pointed "upward" so that God might be entertained by our songs—when instead, we discover that music becomes the way in which God gives to *us*, sends *us* a graceful word, gathers *us* in mercy, and propels *us* to love and serve our neighbor. Music is given to us to proclaim God's saving action in the world. By this proclamation, God is praised. Music, for Luther, is the servant of such praise, forever linked to the proclamation of the truth of our need for God and God's answer to that need in the person of Jesus Christ. It is no surprise to us, then, that Luther would urge the church to use the communally accessible musical form of song. In his day, this expression through music consisted especially of singing the gospel using the rugged "bar-form" of singing—a technical term for the communal art song of the minnesingers[38] and not, despite the widespread modern myth, a reference to songs sung in "bars."

Since the time when these important shapers and reformers taught about music in the church, some potent changes in music have made questions of musical power more complex. Prior to the seventeenth century, most musical forms were thoroughly communal expressions, in which each voice and instrument took an equal part in the full texture of a piece. With the creation of opera and the concerto (which developed almost simultaneously with the rise of Pietism and heightened individualism), human musical fascination became interested in the primacy of solo voices or instruments. In the twentieth century, this pronounced affection for individual musical expression continued and was heightened with the invention of the microphone and recording technology. Amplification makes it possible for one voice or instrument to be heard louder than any other sound. Also, while once music was an art linked to a specific time, now music can be lifted out of time through recordings, and then manipulated, packaged commercially, and sold.

When music participates in an economy in this manner, it takes on the powers of other commercial commodities. Such changes to musical power can be both advantageous and dangerous. Augustine, Ambrose, and Luther, in their critique or embrace of communal song in the Christian assembly could have never anticipated what these musical developments would mean for assembly singing today. Certainly, these innovations forever changed the way we receive and use musical power, particularly musical power in relationship to communal singing in praise of God and proclamation of the word.

Whenever any power is brought to a Christian assembly, we must consider what we will do with such power. Like the powers of privilege that come from class, rank, gender, wealth, or status, musical power must also always yield to the purpose of the assembly. In fact, in a Christian assembly, power is wielded in the way Christ himself is powerful—by being broken. When musical power claims its own reign and pushes aside the center of the assembly, music then becomes a thing to be worshiped and adored, leading us to idolatry. Instead, Christians are continually invited to allow the power of music to be broken to the center of our common worship. Paul Westermeyer helps us to think about the broken nature of music in his book on hymn tunes:

> By "broken to" I mean set next to, contextualized by, made new
> by, transformed by word and sacraments. All art and music, like
> everything from the culture, is in the economy of grace renewed
> and transformed by the gospel. This works itself out not in
> flights of fancy, but in being set next to and thereby transformed
> by the means by which God in Christ through the Holy Spirit
> chooses to address us, namely word and sacraments.[39]

The way in which word and sacraments break the power of music
is the way in which all things are broken in the liturgy—by setting
things side-by-side in tension. For instance, when music is set next
to a ritual action, say, for instance, a procession, the movement of
that procession and the music are transformed, each interpreting the
other. If the music is constructed and performed like a march, the
procession will have a certain march-like character. But the procession may also transform or interpret the music of the march. When
music is set next to, and thereby broken to the means of grace (word
and sacrament), the music and its power are changed. In this trans-
formation, the assembly is able to hear and see the means of grace in
renewed ways. But when music wields its own power, refusing to be
broken, word and sacraments are obscured and blocked, and all that
we see and hear are echoes of our own songs, and not the song of God
rooted in the praise and proclamation of the gospel.

What follows from this proposal is that any who care for and
plan Christian worship must always consider the context of musical expression. Worship planners cannot simply consult a worship
planning guide and chose three hymns to place indiscriminately
throughout a liturgy. Instead, we must all ask deeper questions: Who
will sing this music? How is the assembly—and not a choir, a band,
an organ, or a soloist—the primary musical expression of the liturgy? What is happening while the music is sung or played? What
interpretive devices will be employed to heighten the actions or
symbols held in tension with this music? When the music does not

contain words, what will the instrumental sounds lead the hearer to imagine or feel? In what ways will this music enliven memory, even nostalgia or sentiment, in the assembly? How is this music proclaiming the gospel? How might this music be only a mirror of ourselves and our tastes or desires and thus obscure our encounter with God and God's grace?

Another principal way that Christians can engage in the breaking of musical power to the center of the assembly is by insisting that we always sing more than one kind of music. When worship is made up of only one style or one musical idea, there is a temptation to be drawn to that one expression, entrusting to it a magnified power that diverts our attention from the center. Music from one time and place set next to other music from varied times and places invites us to rejoice in the complexity of the church beyond these variables. A plainchant hymn at the gathering followed soon by a gospel setting of the psalmody followed still later by an Asian hymn of the day will break the power of any one of those styles and draw us to focus on the actions, words, and symbols that root us in the word and sacraments.

Some have argued that a worship book containing many diverse musical settings of holy communion draws unnecessary attention to musical styles. However, one could argue that such diversity points away from stylistic concerns of a particular age or culture and highlights the common shape and language of the liturgy we celebrate together. We engage in the continual breaking of musical power when we sing both local and catholic (i.e., universal) songs, melodies from both here and there, ancient and recent compositions, songs that are at the same time ours and theirs, new and familiar, full of praise and honest with lament, in major and minor modes, with driving rhythm and flowing melody, with organ accompaniment or strings, or brass, or guitars, or drums, or synthesizers, or woodwinds. In light of this diversity, the practice of offering a menu of services with defined musical options on Sunday morning in many congregations (8:15 Chant Liturgy; 9:30 Rock'n'roll; 10:45 Polka Mass) ought to be rethought and, perhaps, discontinued. Instead, music from diverse styles and places will find a home at every liturgy when it is, all of it, broken to the center: the center of worship in word and sacrament—the triune God gathering, speaking, feeding, sending—for the life of the world.

As mentioned earlier, electronic advancements have forever changed the nature of musical power. When a Christian assembly uses music made by electronic means, we must always consider how this music can be broken to the center. In most cases, a solo singer using a microphone does not encourage the assembly to sing but rather urges them to listen. When recordings of music are used in the assembly, such music cannot breathe with, adapt to, or respond to the body gathered in worship. In this way, recordings cannot easily, if at all, be broken to the center. Nor can sequenced synthesizers, which are programmed to play the contents of a major hymnal, truly "lead" assembly song. When we have become so conditioned by our recorded music culture to expect studio quality recordings to stand in for the assembled body of Christ in song (and live human leadership that the assembly needs to make its song), we have placed an unbroken musical power at the center. In these matters, when the broken life of the assembly and its word of life are at stake—we must together say "no."

Elsewhere in this Worship Matters series, Gordon Lathrop used his famous image of a bell in the tower of West Denmark Lutheran Church in Luck, Wisconsin, to focus on the central matters of worship in word and sacrament. This bell, now destroyed, once bore a Danish inscription, which when translated read, "To the bath and the table, the prayers and the word, I call every seeking soul." As was common with bells at that time, the inscription was meant to give words to the toll of the bell, as if the bell could speak or sing. Lathrop used this image to teach the central things: a bath that washes us in mercy and joins us as a body to the saving death of Christ, a table with a meal over which thanks is given and in which all may eat and drink the presence of the living God, prayer for the needs of the world, and the word of God read and interpreted that we might come to know our need for God and God's answer to that need in the life, death, and resurrection of Jesus Christ. The image of the bell is helpful as we sort out what is central and what is peripheral to Christian worship.

Music is not part of the inscription on that bell from Luck, Wisconsin, which calls every seeking soul to word, bath, prayers, and table. But the central things are inscribed on a *bell*, a musical instrument, as if the bell itself were fully aware that the music it makes is strong enough to carry these central things, able to bear the task of making these central things audible and communally received. Music is not a sacrament, and we must say honestly that it is possible to have Christian worship without music. But the power of music is perhaps the strongest vehicle we have for the central matters to be truly evident, and music's contribution to Christian worship is certainly irreplaceable. Twentieth century liturgical scholar Gabe Huck, in *How Can I Keep from Singing?*, states that "musical liturgy is redundant." Indeed, the liturgy itself is a musical event, by virtue of its recurring patterns and the natural way music finds itself to be an expression of the mercy we see in bath, word, prayer, and table. Thus, for hearing-impaired Christians among us, we must say that the fullness of the liturgy is truly present to them when the central matters are present. We plan our liturgies to be musical events, even when some of us cannot hear them, because we know that music causes a thing to happen that no other medium can fully duplicate.

This understanding of musical power broken to the center of Christian worship is perhaps best summed up in an analogy found in the history of architecture. At the end of the Middle Ages, sculptors were able to create works of art in their studios and later install them in the buildings that were being built. Although the art may or may not have fit in with the surrounding architecture or even with the base edifice, the artist enjoyed an amazing freedom in the studio. However, Romanesque sculptors from an earlier period were asked to create their art on site, molding capitals and tympana. In this period, respect for the architectural form was what motivated the imagination. Such respect leads to unity for the whole building. The art was broken to the architecture. The architecture then, in turn, gives value to the art.

The same will be the case when music is broken to the center of Christian worship. Musicians will see themselves as artists sensitive to the flow and shape of the communal event. They will renounce the freedom to create music for the assembly as if the contexts were unimportant. They will resist the temptation to allow music to wield an inappropriate power or to allow the music to afford them an inappropriate personal power or privilege in the assembly. Instead, musicians will delight in using musical power that is broken and integrated into a whole event, like Romanesque columns crafted for an architectural edifice. Elisha's musician made music, and the power of God came and broke the music to a center—God acting to bring something out of nothing. God grant that all music making in the life of the church be broken to such a center, that all of our liturgies may be filled with the life-giving mercy of God.

For reflection and discussion

1. Consider your daily pattern and think about how often you hear music. How much of the daily music that you hear is live music and how much of it is recorded music? Have you noticed differences in the way you listen to live and recorded music?

2. In worship, how have you experienced music to have power? For example, has music enabled you to hear God's word with clarity? If so, when? Has music ever propelled you to respond to God's call, singing to you through the music? If so, how?

3. In worship, have you been aware of times when music has gotten in the way or wielded an inappropriate power? How might such music have been broken to the center?

4. Think of a hymn or song that you sing in worship that comes from a people, time, or place different from your own. How does that song invite you to experience God in a different way or to understand yourself or your assembly in a different way? How and why might you hear the good news in this song?

4
Re-Assembly: Participation as Faith Construction

When Christians meet together for public worship God turns an otherwise ordinary bunch of individuals into a holy nation. Gathering itself is, of course, a response to God's call. The summons has gone out: "Remember the Sabbath day and keep it holy" (Exod. 20:8). The Holy Spirit pulls us in where—as recent worship books put it—God speaks to us, feeds us, blesses us, and sends us out. This is the language *Evangelical Lutheran Worship* uses to explain the pattern for Holy Communion (*Evangelical Lutheran Worship*, pp. 92–93). Gathering starts with God.

In addition to asking what God is doing in our midst on Sunday mornings (or at other times for public worship), we may also ask what it is *we* do when we meet together to honor that call. We have heard God's call, been caught up by it, looked forward to the event, left home, greeted each other, and anticipated the days that will follow until we gather again. Participating in worship is crucial to a life of faith. Participation means that a person becomes a vital part of God's re-assembling the creation that God has made. Out of the many, God makes us one. Out of our brokenness, God has rendered us forgiven and renewed.

Anything said about what *we* do in worship can, of course, sound as if we human beings manufacture the relationship between our creator and us rather than the relationship being God's initiative. Some liturgical scholars helpfully caution us that talking about our *responses* to God's call requires careful nuance. They fear that discussion and execution of plans, especially when labeled *work* (as in "the *work* of the people," one of the ways the Greek word *leitourgia*, or "liturgy," has been understood) leads to a dangerous hubris or even works righteousness. But to speak of what we are doing in worship is not to deny the fundamental and primary action of God. Paying heed to what happens when we assemble for worship is, in fact, to attend to God's gracious action in the world through the central symbols God has given us and to scrutinize the theological assumptions our worship activities express and sustain.

It must be said that one of the symbols of God's grace is the very body of Christ, the assembled people. God gives us to each other. What, then, shall we do together? What does participation in worship really mean? Why is worship important? Why does our participating together in worship matter? What role does the church's witness through word and sacrament play to form us in faith? In many ways, the relationship between what God does in bringing us together and what we do to answer that call is a relationship that feeds on itself. Nevertheless, this essay will focus on what *we* do rather than what God is doing.

Participation cannot result when there is no planning or transparency. One brisk spring evening, I participated in a peace march. Along with about 300 other people, I carried a candle in a large glass (to protect it from the wind) around a small lake in Minnesota. We walked for about 45 minutes, people of all ages and strides, some speaking in whispers or on cell phones, catching-up on neighborhood news, talking politics, or holding silence. As we stretched out around the rim of the lake, our small flames reflected off the water. We could see the evidence of our presence in the light. When we reached the place from which our march had begun, we waited for the trailing end to catch up and then we stood together—huddled, really—outside a stately old park building that served as a backdrop for our statement of peace. We stood in silence, unsure what, if anything, would happen next.

Suddenly the candles and the walking were not enough. A word needed to be placed onto what we had done, to gather up what our presence meant. I ached for someone to read from the prophets or to offer a prayer that might speak so that Jew, Muslim, Christian, people of other faiths, and those without a home in "organized religion" could all have a place *in words* to come together. We needed something to frame our yearning. To be fair, someone did start singing the John Lennon song, "All we are saying is 'Give peace a chance'"—surely an attempt at a common ground—but despite the resonance of its tune in the experience of a previous war, the words seemed naïve. Giving peace a chance was not, in fact, "all we were saying." There was much more to be said, and yet no one had planned what that could be.

Perhaps no one knew how to bring together such a disparate group formed around a single conviction. Perhaps the problem lay in being an *ad hoc* assembly in a culture with an increasing lack of ritual sense. And even more, none of us could prepare to participate beyond bringing candles and wearing sturdy shoes for the walk. No one else could step in because we had no agreement on who could—or whether anyone ought to—take on that role. Maybe we were all a bit shy, too.

When the holy people gather on Sunday morning (or another time scheduled for worship), we do not have to come unprepared and unable to participate fully. We do not have to be left out in the cold, hungering for a word or song that could deepen our communal identity. We best arrive for—and depart from—an event whose pattern we know ahead of time, where the expectations have come to reside in our bones, and where we can take part.

What is participation?

Current talk about participation

Participation is much discussed in the church. Leonard Sweet, a popular critic of the "modern" church, insists that participation is critical to turning around the so-called demise (membership losses) of the mainline churches.[40] "Unless mainline churches can transition their worship," he writes, "into more EPIC directions—Experiential, Participatory, Image-Based, and Communal—they stand the real risk of becoming museum churches, nostalgic testimonies to a culture that is no more."[41] Sweet advocates that worship appeal to "postmodern" sensibilities by marketing itself to the needs of people who welcome (1) interactive experience, (2) the power of metaphor for its window into complex ideas, (3) narrative for its ability to create context for communal identity, and (4) the opportunity to serve others.

There is much to appreciate in Sweet's list of goals for worship. Really participating in worship engages us through metaphor and image into a new identity as a community of service for the sake of the world. Even in the goals Sweet lists for healthy postmodern churches, notice that participation is about being formed into a new community whose gaze is outward toward service.

Yet, this is not quite the same sense of participation as Sweet endorses elsewhere in his book. He speaks, for instance, of participation as the need among postmoderns to "hold the mike themselves."[42] Along with other language that refers to worship as a marketing tool, this desire to perform easily undercuts the primacy of Christ and the community he forms by assuaging the individual's clamor for attention. If worship were an outlet for self-expression, then we would need to ask whether worship has much to do with faithfulness or even Christ. Further, if worship is used as an antidote to decline in churches, it readily becomes a marketing tool. In other words, worship then becomes something other than worship.

A few years ago I had a conversation with a pastor who was intent on the people in the congregation "participating" in what was going on in worship. She mentioned the rise in the number of people who volunteered to sing a solo or play music with a group. More people were willing to stand up in front of others and say something: give a "temple talk" or sermon or make an announcement. This pastor's notion of "participation" meant making room for individuals to do something special, to share their gifts with the others in the congregation, to enhance the worship experience. Worship was to be friendly and accessible so that no one should feel uncomfortable or alienated.

These ways of including people in worship can, indeed, offer the impression that the worship is participatory. The danger is that they can also trivialize participation by defining it as something an individual might do now and then rather than something expected of everyone all the time. Participation is not about dressing the bones but about *being* the bones. It is the difference between having the children come up front to sing so the people can see them and having the children lead the singing of a psalm as worship leaders who are not on display. It is the difference between holding the mike and, more preferably, supporting the congregation's own singing. These distinctions are not easy to make because they can be quite subtle. How do we draw the line between one way of participating and another?

A deeper meaning of participation
Participation is about the whole assembly being engaged in the depth of God's meaning through encounter with the means of grace: the word of God (the scriptures read and preached) and the sacraments of baptism and holy communion. Gordon Lathrop reminds us that "the symbols of the meeting are not a code, each symbol having a single significance and a code book giving the translation. They are rather a lively and multivalent language, the meaning resident in the experienced participation in the whole event."[43] Participation is not about being up in front of everyone but being with everyone in the presence of the grace and mercy of God.

"Participate" is an old word from the French, *participare*, meaning "to impart a share," so that what we "participate" in is something in which we "take part," "have a part or a share." The *Oxford English Dictionary* says it is "to possess or enjoy in common with others." Is that not what God has given us—an inheritance with all the saints, a share in the kingdom, a place at the table? These are mysteries in the midst of God's sure and certain promise of their reality.

As you can see, to participate is, in the deepest sense, not so much about giving as it is receiving. It isn't so much about singing a solo as it is to hear others' voices; not so much getting everybody's attention as receiving your share with all the others. But in fact, it is both to give and to receive for it is to take a part (in all the ambiguity of that phrase).

Participation means operating as subjects, not objects. When we realize what the worship will entail, we come ready to absorb what lies inside and is revealed through its pattern and content (its form and substance, in other terms). The availability of *Evangelical Lutheran Worship* and other such worship books—actual print on paper that is available for all participants to hold and use—makes worship a thoroughly knowable event. Patterns that come to be familiar in the bones of the people are the most democratic of all. Participation demands transparency. When we know ahead of time what is going to happen, what the focus will be, what will be asked of us, what we can expect of our leaders and neighbors, we can know the purpose of the gathering and take our places as active partakers in it rather than as passive observers.

In worship, faith is formed by the ways in which the people encounter one another and the symbols of our faith. We sit together in the presence of God's word read and preached. We pray together with people whose perspectives we disliked when we heard them over coffee the week before. We end up practicing the experiences that our scriptures hold out to us as goals: in Christ there is no east or west, no male nor female, no slave nor free. Hearing that word, we find ourselves as the Levite *and* the Samaritan *and* the one who was left by the side of the road. By the pattern of gathering and hearing the word, we are invited to absorb a way of being that runs counter to the defensive or self-promoting postures of the marketplace, for instance. In worship, no person or skill has greater value than another. All members are needed equally in the body of Christ. All need and are fed an equal share in the realm of God's mercy.

Our encounter with the symbols of God's grace forms faith in modes beyond the rational. In worship, you don't simply grasp a thing with reason; you encounter and "try on" a way of seeing and being that, by being infused into you over a period of time—a lifetime, say—has its way with you. Princeton philosopher, Kwame Anthony Appiah, who grew up in Ghana and who has straddled culture and ethnicity all his life, writes that:

> I believe in reason. But I have learned in a life of university teaching and research that even the cleverest people are not easily shifted by reason alone—and that can be true even in the most cerebral of realms. One of the great savants of the post-war era, John von Neumann, liked to say, mischievously, that "in mathematics you don't understand things, you just get used to them."[44]

In worship, we don't just grasp Christian faith with our reasoning. We don't just hear a doctrinal proposition or an exhortation to a particular behavior and give our lives to it. Although some people may come to faith in cerebral ways, it is exceptional. For most of us, and for most of our lives, we continually try on promises from God that are incredible, unbelievable. When Jesus healed the epileptic child, the child's father said to Jesus, "I believe; help my unbelief!" (Mark 9:24), a description of the Christian life cherished by Martin Luther. We never can understand these things. Perhaps we can only get used to them.

What we do together is not salvific. Obviously, none of this discussion has a thing to do with whether one's relationship with God is "good enough." Nothing we *do* on Sunday morning is going to make us acceptable to God, who welcomes us at the center of worship. And yet we can have conversation about what we do on Sunday morning because we are free to do one thing or another.

In fact, we must have conversation about our choices because some proposals for change in worship suggest that worship is meant to be a vehicle for healing all that ails the church in any age. The bandwagon of criticisms about complacent worship leaders who seem to go through the motions perfunctorily often sounds like the answer is to put more personality into the worship, "be different," or present a less complex faith without odd symbols like the cross or the empty tomb. Sometimes the solution to fears that attendance is declining due to worship practices proposes that the problem is "sacramental elitism," with the solution being to dispense with baptism as the initiatory sacrament into the body of Christ. In other words, as it is argued in some quarters, people should not have to be baptized in order to be welcome at the table. And further, the solution to the problem of people perceiving the church to be too rigidly hierarchical is to do away with any and all differentiation of callings in the assembly; let everyone take turns preaching the word and administering the sacraments.

Whether the issue is real or imagined, being able to participate fully in worship is not a "fix" for a problem. Participatory worship is much more than an answer to a problem. Problems are dilemmas for which a solution can be found. Problems have answers. The question for which worship is an appropriate response is much deeper than a problem. That question is the crisis of being human. Problems, in other words, have solutions; crises require presence. Worship is the presence of the triune God for a people formed by gathering around the media that make God's word visible and audible. Worship is the means by which we are formed to live by faith in the crisis that is life; for worship is made up of the gifts that do save us, gifts given by God: word, water, bread, and wine.

Worship present to itself—worship without ulterior purposes
Worship choices need to be about what is most faithful. The choices set before us are many, and the voices that mean to give the best advice on how Sunday morning should be done (some people use words such as *exciting, dynamic, mission-oriented*) can set us on a path that leads to greater or lesser faithfulness. The danger, however, is not in talking about what is to be done. Rather, the danger lies in failing to see that worship conducted for an ulterior purpose—for something other than worship—is worship that has gone astray. If worship does not intend to be significant in the present, it has lost its point, its center.

An "ulterior" motive is one that is kept hidden. Nothing is what it seems to be. The point of the event is not its present time but an outcome meant to bear fruit at another time. *Now*, in other words, is for later. The focus, then, of the Sunday morning worship will not be *this* morning's worship but some future moment with some ulterior outcome. The ends justify the means because the future goal determines the present event rather than the presence of Christ *now* taking center stage. Worship cannot function as a means to an end other than itself, for faith is not formed *now* in the future; it is nurtured week by week in the present assembly, the event of God's speaking and feeding and sending the people *now*.

Eugene Brand, whose liturgical scholarship was critical to *Lutheran Book of Worship*, often used the word *edify* when referring to faithful worship. Worship should be "edifying." This use of the word could sound too rational and too utilitarian, but Brand meant it in another vein. He was concerned for the building-up of the body of Christ. Instead of thinking of good worship practices as those that conform to some unalterable form determined by ecclesiastical police, Brand held that good worship is what best constructs the body of Christ.

> Lutheran worship has tended to be either improperly clericalized by advocates among the restorationists of the so-called

high church position, or improperly declericalized by those who misunderstood the doctrine of the priesthood of all believers. One finds few places where the congregation has become fully involved in the celebration of Holy Communion *and* where the proper role of the ordained clergy in preaching and presiding is understood and maintained. One encounters either the "Herr Pastor" or the "my mass" type of clericalist monopoly, or one encounters the "anyone may do anything" kind of egalitarianism.[45]

A little further on, Brand wrote that the goal for renewal of the Sunday morning worship is that the "pastor is neither the celebrant nor the liturgist; the pastor presides over a congregation involved in celebrating the liturgy."[46] Everyone is meant to be involved. In other words, worship is not a task performed by the pastor or worship leaders; it is not a performance at all.

Worship is not a perfunctory obligation that must simply be endured by an audience observing from a distance. Rather, worship is a corporate action; the congregation, led by the pastor and worship leaders (most of whom are lay members of the congregation), together listen to and feed on the promises of God, give thanks, and articulate the needs of the world, begging for wisdom and healing. By sound and physical movement the assembly "assembles" the event. There are no bystanders. The assembly gathers, engages with the word of God as it is made audible and visible in and to themselves—the body of Christ—and in language, images, water, and food, and then the assembly is sent out.

Worship is primary formation in faith
Sunday morning is foundational.[47] Truly participatory worship holds that what is done on Sunday morning sits at the foundation of what the church is all about because it is the place of public proclamation of the word of God. One highly respected New Testament scholar in

the ELCA, Arland Hultgren, tells his classes at Luther Seminary in St. Paul, Minnesota, that "worship precedes scripture." He means that the Bible's contents (the books chosen by the church to be included in the Bible) grew out of the writings that the first Christians found to be consistently nurturing for them in their faith.

This same idea is central to Sandra Schneiders's important book on interpreting scripture, *The Revelatory Text*. As a New Testament scholar and professor of Christian spirituality, she writes: "the relationship between tradition and scripture is that of a hermeneutical dialectic. Scripture is produced as part of and witness to tradition."[48]

As the letters of Paul, the earliest writings of what became the New Testament, traveled from church to church in the early decades of the church's life, their wisdom and challenge found a home among the churches. People wanted to hear these writings. They wanted to hear the law and the prophets, too, and to sing the songs they had learned in the synagogue, the psalms (the Psalter). The story of the compilation of the Bible's contents is complex, but it entailed much discernment on the part of the churches—the first Christian theologians—to determine which writings were consistent with an overarching biblical theology that upheld the majesty, grace, and paradox of the triune God. The history of the church councils (especially Nicea in AD 325 and Chalcedon in AD 451) shows us the wealth of arguments and the carefully nuanced answers that our ancestors wrestled out of the biblical text. But apart from the important place of the word of God in worship on Sunday morning—in the liturgies of baptism and holy communion—the councils would have had little to debate, for the scope and limits of God's written word come out of worship.

From the beginning, liturgical historians tell us, people gathered on Sunday morning. We have a few, precious historical documents that lay out what may have been done, although written documents cannot show us whether the churches carried out what the documents said should be done. We also have no reason to insist that we should do what we guess our ancestors might have done in worship. No liturgical historian or liturgical theologian has made the case—or even intends to make the case—that the church's worship must imitate a golden age of worship if such were ever to be found.[49]

Yet, we do know what some documents tell us. The Didache, which some scholars think may even go back to sources as early as AD 50, contains instructions about what is said at a baptism and what is said over the bread and the wine, and all of it is remarkably similar to what the churches say even today.[50]

Justin Martyr's description in his *First Apology*[51] from about AD 150 is written to the emperor describing what Christians do on Sunday morning in order to plead that the emperor stop tormenting them. He says that the people come together on "the day of the Sun" to hear the prophets and the apostles read "as long as time allows." Then the presider gives thanks over the bread and wine, remembering Jesus, and finally they give money for the poor. Some of that text was printed in the introductory pages of *With One Voice* along with other writings from throughout the centuries to help place the pattern of worship laid out in *With One Voice* within its historical trajectory.[52] The point was to help the church see itself as standing in a long line of ancestors whose way of passing on the faith has held to certain crucial pieces: gathering, word, meal, sending.

Other documents show us in even more detail what certain worship services and rites included. The Apostolic Tradition of, perhaps, AD 315 is a compilation of a number of services that looks like a how-to manual for the churches: how to baptize, teach, or catechize, how to hold holy communion, how to bless and ordain, when to pray, and the like. Although the origin and purpose of these writings remain shrouded in mystery, they nevertheless exist as tantalizing glimpses of diverse persons' representations of Christian worship at certain points in history. It is astounding to see the commonality among even these writings from so many centuries ago.

Why are these discoveries so exciting? Seeing where we have come from, what we still hold dear, is a window into a mystery no human beings have fully captured. We live into our faith along with our ancestors. We do not have a worshiping faith that is formed out of nothing or only out of today's cultural preferences. Only God can create out of the void. We human beings create and maintain out of tradition, albeit one that has been handed to us from our Creator through our fellow creatures.

Tradition matters

On the one hand, we live in a time of disinterest or even distrust in tradition. A prominent myth in the culture of the United States is that this culture tossed away tradition in favor of what is new and up-to-date. The seemingly endless frontier opened up the chance to start afresh and leave behind what, for some people, begged to be forgotten. That the United States is a nation of immigrants has meant that traditions have had to be bent or to change into something acceptable to the neighbors. Adapt or die. Reform or be left behind. We have lived according to slogans and dicta of progress that leave little room for "the old ways."

On the other hand, hunger for a tie to what came before remains with us. Look at some of the newest twenty-first-century housing developments that sport front porches, streets you can walk along to get to the corner grocery, or neighborhood community spaces meant to boost the old ways of being neighbors. Some call it nostalgic; others, a move toward calm (or sensible energy use) in a fast-paced world. What is happening in these new constructs is a recognition that some of what came before us shaped a healthy way of being in relationship with one another on our streets and neighborhoods and a way of slowing down to give time to physical activities such as sports and gardening. Something in the "old" way of being together had value beyond what has replaced it. Even more than that, the recognition that a certain "sanity" requires actual physical accommodation—attention to spaces, proximities, ways in which we move through the world—is an endorsement of the fact that how we see, what we know, has something to do with what we actually *do*.

The tradition handed down by any human endeavor—whether family, church, or state—is riddled with the potential to be either constructive or destructive. We make choices all the time about what we will continue to observe and pass on to the next generation and what we will alter or stop doing. But what is needed for making those crucial choices is knowledge of the core of the event. Any single experience—an anecdotal account of worship in one congregation or in one of the many traditions of the church or in one version of the church's tradition—does not teach enough about the larger picture to allow for informed choices.

As mentioned previously, Schneiders's work deals in part with the relationship between scripture and tradition but then moves on to distinguish between tradition (singular) and traditions (plural). Traditions include the diversity of experiences people encounter in worship everywhere on a Sunday morning. It is natural for people who are familiar only with their own congregations to think that what is provincial is best or even universal. What people experience locally, however, is often only one of many traditions (plural). When we get used to certain ways and certain modes of operating, we assign meaning to those modes. It is a short jump, then, to believing that whatever the quirks of the local congregation (one's own province, so to speak), the faith itself is best expressed and absorbed through those traditions.

Because worship is about more than the rational mind's agreement about an idea, the ways in which we engage with the forms of our worship have a great deal to do with what we believe. What we do reflects what we believe. As Appiah puts it,

> The connection people feel to cultural objects that are symbolically theirs, because they were produced from within a world

of meaning created by their ancestors—the connection to art through identity—is powerful. It should be acknowledged. The cosmopolitan, though, wants to remind us of other connections. One connection—the one neglected in talk of cultural patrimony—is the connection not *through* identity but *despite* difference.[53]

Liturgical renewal is about recovery of tradition, and it is, in the best sense, cosmopolitan. Rather than finding our faith by asserting diversity, liturgical tradition (singular) recognizes a core built of many divergent strands and even opposing, or at least paradoxical, theological interpretations. Out of the clash of oppositions (for example: Jesus Christ as both truly human and truly divine) has come to us the strong heart of Christian witness and worship. It can wear many different kinds of music and colors and rhythms, but it needs the assembly to "assemble" it.

The renewal movement for worship has been going on for more than 140 years.[54] What began as interest in history became over the course of time a vibrant call to investigate and discover the work of God in every age of the church's worship life. From the history of worship, liturgical scholars made some proposals about how we all might rethink and reconfigure worship by seeing ourselves as people beholden to what has been handed to us and what we have been entrusted to hold out for others. According to Schneiders, while tradition has often been referred to in ecumenical circles and doctrinal debates as a repetition of what could be perceived as a fixed entity (dogma), tradition in fact "refers to the sum total of appropriated and transmitted Christian experience." Out of the rich treasure of its tradition, Christians throughout history have selected the material for renewed syntheses of faith.[55] "To qualify as tradition does not mean to be a repetition of apostolic tradition. It means to be in living continuity with it."[56] Liturgical renewal has meant to unveil the tradition of apostolic witness and faith in Christ Jesus.

A few liturgical changes, already familiar to most people, heighten such participation. These changes make clear that:

1. Worship should be conducted in the language of the people so that everyone can understand what is being said. The particularity of a place and a time has to be honored. This could even mean paying attention to some of the generational differences in the language used for the worship.

2. Worship should be conducted by the people gathered for worship. Everything that is sung should be played and vocalized "live," that is, there should be no audio or even visual aspects that come "canned" from elsewhere. Rather, the people should participate as fully as possible in all aspects of worship: singing, speaking, and even decorating the worship space. As much as possible, all aspects for worship should come from those who are physically present.

3. The most fundamental basis on which the worship on a given Sunday is formed—that of the word of God for that day—needs to be owned by the people. This common ownership is accomplished through the use of a lectionary—especially the Revised Common Lectionary, which supports attention to the ecumenically observed liturgical year.

4. People from the entire assembly ought to help lead the worship in every part that is not specifically stipulated as a task for those set apart for the public ministry of word and sacrament. The prayers ought to be locally crafted for each specific time and place. The readings should come through divergent voices. In everything but preaching (word) and presiding at the Lord's supper, lay people may take part, lead, and do the work of the worship.[57]

In short, participation is about emphasizing the broadest possible involvement of and ownership by the assembly in worship. It does not mean that we do away with ordaining people who are called by a congregation to serve as public ministers of word and sacrament. It is necessary for there to be people who are placed in such positions. But those who hold such positions also need to understand that the gift of the Sunday morning event is that it brings people together to hear, eat, and go out—in short, to *do* something. It is an active experience of a people. It is not the gathering of an audience for a show. Participation cuts short inappropriate clergy power by making the priesthood we hold in Christ with all believers a stronger reality.

Sometimes, even failure to use a standard lectionary can undermine participation by the people. It is ironic how some congregations that talk most about being "participatory" often leave major worship decisions to the pastor or the worship committee. When the common lectionary (or an alternate lectionary) is not used on a regular basis, it often means that the most fundamental cornerstone regarding the word from God that will be heard in the assembly—how Jesus will be present—is left to the whims of a few. To be sure, a particularly traumatic event, for example, may cause the pastor to add to the appointed readings or change them. However, what is the result when the people arrive for worship only then to discover what readings have been assigned? When the people do not know ahead of time what the scripture basis is for the worship, they cannot have read them ahead of time in order to prepare themselves for worship. No one can have practiced to be the scripture reader, the lector. They cannot have thought through what hymn texts or what music, what tunes, what musical keys, might best help "say" what the texts say. The one who is designated as the intercessor cannot prepare prayers that connect with the scripture readings and the liturgical day, for lectionary and calendar are intrinsically related. When you cannot prepare, you cannot fully participate. Worship easily becomes a show to watch or, worse, a place to be manipulated rather than a gathering in which to participate.

Why is participation so important? Participation is the way in which we come to live the faith that has been passed on from our ancestors. It is not the faith of any one group but is the sum total—or the crux—of what others have seen and heard about the triune God. It is not owned by any particular racial, ethnic, or identity group. Evidence is in the prayers and the hymns that have their origin in one church but are prayed and sung in many others. There are no longer "Methodist hymns" or "Anglican hymns" or "Lutheran hymns," and so on, but all the songs of faith that accord with the texts and themes for a given Sunday are appropriate to sing.[58] Scripture readings do not belong to any one theological realm, but all are passed along for the building up—the edification—of the church.

What the assembly enacts on Sunday morning is a pattern that has come to us from long ago, nurtured through the centuries, fought over, changed, denied, revised, amended, and continually reformed by the Holy Spirit among all sorts of Christians caught in the very act of encountering the one holy God, the God-with-us, Emmanuel. What our churches do on a given Sunday is to take a part in the pattern of the ages. In so doing, we make history as well, and we do so *out* of the history that has formed us.

We are called by God to participate in the gifts of worship. Indeed, the apostle Paul wrote about this calling in 1 Corinthians 10:16-17, in order to connect God's presence and our participation in worship. "The cup of blessing that we bless, is it not a participation (Greek: *koinonia*) in the blood of Christ? The bread that we break, is it not a participation (Greek: *koinonia*) in the body of Christ? Because there is one bread, we who are many are one body, for we all partake of the one bread." Truly, this participation in worship is the most remarkable, and central, of all.

For reflection and discussion

1. How did you first become familiar with Christian faith? Who (or what) were your first teachers and how did they "teach" you?

2. How do you participate in worship at the church you now attend? Did you engage in worship differently in other congregations? What made the difference?

3. Discuss the ways you participate at a sporting event even as a spectator, a musical concert, a dance, a movie theater, a county fair, or the voting booth. Think of describing each experience in terms of its ritual actions. What do they have in common? How are they different?

4. What is the most important part of Sunday worship for you and why?

5. What was the most memorable worship service you have experienced? Can you also tell about worship that was the least nourishing or the most maddening? Discuss why each of these experiences struck you as they did.

6. Does your congregation have a tradition that you would like to see ended or have you experienced a worship practice elsewhere that you wish your congregation would adopt? What is it? What would it take to change things?

5
Worship at the Edges: Redefining Evangelism

The sending

The distribution of holy communion is coming to a close and we are singing Simeon's song from Luke 2, the *Nunc dimittis* (Now, Lord, you let your servant go in peace). We have seen with our own eyes the salvation of God, given to us in the bread and wine, given to us in and through the community. The pastor or lay minister distributing the food to those gathered around the table has spoken with a loud voice, audible for all to hear: "The body of Christ, given for you." For we remember that the body of Christ given "for you" and the blood shed "for you" centers us, so to speak, in a community, in a communal sharing. It invites us into a communal identity, not an individual, private, self-focused centering. The scriptural "for you" is plural.

We have concluded the sharing of the body and the blood of the Christ. We have all, in bodily gesture or in our heart, knelt or bowed to receive that sacrament. We have all become what we have received—the body of Christ.

And now we come to the fourth and last part of the Sunday pattern for worship—the sending. "God blesses us and sends us in mission to the world" (*Evangelical Lutheran Worship*, p. 93). Perhaps several

ministers of communion have been entrusted with the remaining elements from communion "to take to those who are absent from the
assembly" (*Evangelical Lutheran Worship* Leaders Edition, p. 24). A
prayer may have been said over these ministers and for those who
will receive communion from them. Announcements have been made
"especially those related to the assembly's participation in God's mission in the world" (*Evangelical Lutheran Worship*, p. 114). Perhaps
an affirmation of Christian vocation has been used recognizing particular vocations of service in the church or service to the world—
an affirmation, in a sense, of the various ways in which people live
out their baptism (*Evangelical Lutheran Worship* Leaders Edition, p.
25). The blessing has been spoken and now, as we sing the sending
song, people wait for the "dismissal." We come to the last dialogue
of our Sunday liturgy. We await the words—"Go in peace. Serve the
Lord. Thanks be to God!"—and yet, these words appear sometimes
so insignificant that we hardly notice them. Perhaps we are simply
glad that the service has come to an end (that it is finally over!), or
perhaps we are already thinking about the coffee hour (because we
sure are getting thirsty!), or perhaps we are thinking about what else
we still have to do today. We look at our watches. We barely take note
of this concluding dialogue other than as a sign that the service is
finished—that we are "dismissed." And yet in this exchange we are
actually summarizing everything that has happened in the pattern of
worship we have celebrated. In these two phrases, we are preparing
the ground for the continuation of the liturgy into the world—the
"liturgy after the liturgy."

Evangelical Lutheran Worship offers us several options for this
sending dialogue. "Go in peace. Remember the poor," or "Go in peace.
Share the good news," or "Go in peace. Christ is with you," and of
course "Go in peace. Serve the Lord." Each of these liturgical exchanges
affirms the pattern of worship in which we have just participated. And
with our resounding response, "Thanks be to God," we, too, affirm
that this pattern is for the world. This pattern has welcomed our story,

our lives, and now gives us orientation in the world. We are sent out into the world as part of God's mission.

What has this sending to do with the "center" that has been the focus of this little volume? We all know that "centers" can be dangerous things. Many abuses can be inflicted on individuals and communities because of a perceived "center" that becomes normative. Liturgists have been particularly susceptible to the temptation of establishing a nearly tyrannical center that must be observed without question. Curiously enough, those who have opposed renewal in worship or have argued against those reflecting on the rituals often establish their own tyrannical centers. They have fallen prey to the same temptation.

This temptation is always to make the "center" about us. Worship becomes about us. The Bible and its message become about us (that is, the Bible agrees with everything we like and disagrees with everything we disdain). Of course, this all-about-me focus is not the intent of our use of the word *center* or *centripetal* in the writing of this book. Timothy Wengert has already noted (p. 23), "at the fringes, we encounter the center. And, at the center, the fringes." And again, citing Gordon Lathrop, Christian worship is about the center and the edges.

The center, in other words, does not exist without the edges. We could argue that the edges will always be there—the reality of human existence with its joys and its pains, with its tensions and contradictions, with its compromises and failings, with its surprises and its tragedies; the reality of suffering in the world, of useless suffering, inexplicable suffering of communities and peoples. The edges are always with us. But the center, Jesus Christ proclaimed as crucified and risen, can never be centripetal if it is not also at the edge.

Whenever we want to forget this characteristic of all centers, whenever we want to establish a center as definitive (even when we claim that center to be God—and perhaps especially then), we only fall into the trap about which Martin Luther already warned us. We are simply erecting a new altar to a God whom we have invented.

Nevertheless, God says: "I do not choose to come to you in My majesty and in the company of angels but in the guise of a poor beggar asking for bread." You may ask: "How do you know this?" Christ replies: "I have revealed to you in My Word what form I would assume and to whom you should give. You do not ascend into heaven, where I am seated at the right hand of My heavenly Father, to give Me something; no, I come down to you in humility. I place flesh and blood before your door with the plea: Give Me a drink! Instead, you want to erect a convent for Me."[59]

The pattern of worship, the celebration of word and sacrament—at least as we argue it in this book—is a "pattern" that is continually broken open. It is a center that directs us to the edges. This pattern points us to the other who, by his or her appearance in our midst (for example, as a beggar) somehow, points out the failure of our often insular and hermetically sealed rituals. We become not only attentive to but also responsible for the cry of the other. It continually makes us aware of the other, our neighbor, in his or her need and of ourselves at the edges. In other words, the "center" is about sending us out into the world. Let us reflect more on the center and the edges before approaching the complex topic of evangelism or mission.

Center broken open

A less well-known comment from Luther helps us understand the notion of "center" or even of "pattern" as it is used in *Evangelical Lutheran Worship*. It is found in the *Treatise on the New Testament, That Is the Holy Mass*, written in 1520.

Christ, in order to prepare for himself an acceptable and beloved people, which should be bound together in unity through love, abolished the whole law of Moses. And that he might not give further occasion for divisions and sects, he appointed in return but one law or order for his entire people, and that was the holy mass. ... Henceforth, therefore, there is to be no other external order for the service of God except the mass.[60]

What surprises us is Luther's use of the word *law* here in relation to the celebration of holy communion (or mass). How is he using this word? Could he be establishing a new legalistic "center" for worship? Yet, the fact that Luther had an aversion to law is nowhere clearer than in his writings on the liturgy. Despite his deep commitment to basic reformation insights such as communion in two kinds (bread and wine) and the accessibility of communion (as opposed to private masses), when these insights were "forced" upon the people during his absence from Wittenberg, Luther left his "protective custody" at the Wartburg Castle, risking his life, to restore the old order of the Catholic mass. Why? Because he was afraid that the reforming insights were being made into new principles or laws and that the people, rather than being helped, were being confused. Even fundamental evangelical priorities were not to become a new law or new *centers*.

And yet, he writes, there is one law, one order for the whole people. A cursory reading of Luther may leave us perplexed. On the one hand, for example, he argues in 1520 that all the frills—the singing, the organ playing, the bells, vestments, the ornaments, and all the gestures—are human inventions and have nothing to do with holy communion as it was celebrated by Jesus. And then, in a letter from 1539, when responding to a good friend in Brandenburg who was at a loss about how to respond to his sovereign's demand for all those "smells and bells," Luther responds that the prince can process as many times as he wants—as long as the word is proclaimed.[61]

Luther demonstrates a radical freedom with regards to the liturgical enactment of the word because, I believe, he has two presuppositions always before him: first is an inner dynamic, an inner grammar, a center or pattern if you will; and secondly, this pattern is not confined to what happens during the one or two hours that worship is celebrated because this pattern, this grammar, is a grammar for living.

Worship is not to be confined to just the service on Sunday morning but actually forms the pattern of our lives in the world. The center is continually sent out to the edges.

The order that is the "holy mass"[62] is not a new set of rules or principles—no matter how much we wish it were and no matter how much easier that may seem to make our lives. The order is not a new law or center but a language that sends us out and orients us in the world.

The liturgical movement outward is embodied in Luther's *Treatise on the Blessed Sacrament of the Holy and True Body of Christ, and the Brotherhoods*.[63] Here, Luther argues outward from the Sacrament of the Altar. Holy communion is truly a *communio* (Greek: *synaxis*) that, when received, forms a fellowship, a communion, a community. The signs of the sacrament—bread and wine—signify this fellowship. For example, just as the bread is made out of many grains mixed together, each losing its form but taking "upon itself the common body of the bread … so it is and should be with us." The fellowship consists in the happy exchange: Christ taking upon himself our form, which in turn "enkindles in us such love that we take on his form, rely upon his righteousness, life and blessedness."[64] But that is not all. We tend to overlook another part of this so-called happy exchange.

> Again through this same love, we are to be changed and to make the infirmities of all other Christians our own; we are to take upon ourselves their form and their necessity, and all the good that is within our power we are to make theirs, that they may profit from it. That is the real fellowship, and that is the true significance of this sacrament.[65]

The sacrament as real fellowship invites us into a different "grammar" of life—one in which communion with my neighbor, the other, is equated with my own communion in Jesus Christ. It is noteworthy that in this treatise on the Sacrament of the Altar Luther also deals with the subject of "brotherhoods." In the late Middle Ages, the "brotherhoods" were, among other things, to be a special "fraternity" dedicated to doing good works and helping others (perhaps something akin to our charitable organizations). Instead, Luther points out, they are full of gluttony and drunkenness where the moneys collected go only to the maintenance of the group.[66]

On the contrary, the "real fellowship" would "gather provisions and feed and serve a tableful or two of poor people, for the sake of God."[67] The pattern witnessed in the sharing of the bread and the wine, the pattern of God's grace toward us, is lived out in the world and not simply within our local community. This distinction is important. We can all share to some degree within our local parish community. We can all pledge part of our income. We can all donate our time. We can all bring something to eat to the potluck supper (Lutherans are particularly good at this!). But the "real fellowship" is with those who are *not* like us. Luther calls them the poor—the ones who do not have enough to eat. We might call them the poor too, but we may also call them the homeless person, the immigrant, the single mom, the addict. We might also call them those who are in spiritual, physical, or mental distress—the bereaved, the sick, those in anguish, the disabled—all those suffering and in need within our communities. Are they at our table or are we like the "brotherhoods"? Is the table an open center?

Evangelism

We finally come to the word that is to be our main consideration: *evangelism*. The sending from the center is intimately connected to an understanding of evangelism far more inviting than the way we often use the word. The sending, as we have seen, pushes us out of the center toward the edges as people who have received Christ in the happy exchange. This exchange forms us into a pattern of life where we are all at the edges. There no longer are insiders and outsiders.

When we speak of the sending in the pattern of worship, we are talking about the relationship between the liturgy and what we do with the rest of our lives. There is a "grammar" in Christian worship that takes us beyond the concepts and structures we assimilate in our respective cultures and even particular faith expressions. Worship that witnesses to the center—the promised presence of Jesus Christ—is worship that witnesses to the edges, to Jesus Christ in the poor and suffering. In other words, it witnesses to a God who is not found in the heavenly realms but to Christ who declares, "I am in the poor" and "You are the poor." Worship that witnesses to the center involves assemblies in this reorientation—a reorientation of cultural values and theological presuppositions. Evangelism is one of them.

Evangelism has, for a long time, been understood as proclaiming the good news to those who have not heard it—to the "unreached" or to the "unchurched." It presupposes, however, that our center is the center for everyone else. It presupposes that we have "God" whereas others do not. Classical understandings of evangelism establish a strong center that really does not need the edges other than to bring them into the center. It is no wonder that in earlier ages of the church evangelism in the Third World and among the poor was often confused with the political goals of European colonizers.

As Paul Rajashekar has stated in his contribution to *The Evangelizing Church: A Lutheran Contribution*, "it is unhelpful to use the language of 'unreached' to refer to people who are not Christian by faith. It sort of begs the question, 'Unreached by whom'? It does not mean that God has not reached them. It is a fundamental Christian conviction that God's love is *universal* and embraces all people, whether they acknowledge it or not."[68] Evangelism, then, exists in this tension between God's universal love and the particular love of God toward humanity manifest in the cross and resurrection of Jesus Christ.

Proclamation of the word in and through the pattern of worship helps navigate that tension. There is the particular proclamation of God's love distributed in the bread and wine but there is also the breaking-open of the closed circle around the altar when those who have received bread and wine hear the beggar knocking at the door asking for bread. "I am," God states in Luther's words, "that beggar."

Of course, Luther is here thinking of Matthew 25 ("just as you did it to one of the least of these who are members of my family, you did it to me"). But the move outward, the move to the edges, has far-reaching implications for evangelism. The most significant of these is a redrawing of the boundaries between who is in and who is out, who is "reached" and who is "unreached." John F. Hoffmeyer has also proposed this redrawing of the boundaries. Writing specifically about mission, he states, "Unfortunately, the church's thinking about its mission has often been shaped by gap-bridging models. We have too often conceived mission as taking the word of God 'out' into the world, as if the word were not already present in the world."[69] A dangerous model of two realms, of insiders and outsiders, arises.[70]

Luther's understanding of the God who meets us in the beggar asking for bread disrupts the two realms we create. The beggar disrupts the center—any center—we attempt to establish. Luther's understanding of the celebration of holy communion as a real fellowship in which we take upon ourselves the suffering and infirmities of our neighbor—making them our own—disrupts the closed circles we attempt to construct. We cannot hide behind a "them and us" mentality. We are lost if we attempt to defend imaginary lines drawn between the suffering in the world and our lives in Christian communities. The believer is sent out into the world: "Go in peace. Remember the poor." Believers go out, sent as the body of Christ. But in the world they find Christ already there. They find Christ disseminated in the poor, the suffering, the dejected . . . Christ already in the world.

The "one law" (namely, the sacrament of bread and wine) embeds within it a blurring of the boundaries that results in a kind of "displacement" of the bread, body, life, and even God. In the displacement of God's very self into the world (just as the bread is distributed), we, the participants, are awakened to a joyous and free possibility for response. The "service of God" as holy communion—"the real fellowship"—engages us through worship to live out our lives in the world.

Worship, as witness to the center, witnesses to this response—continually sending us out of any closed circle, out of the community, displaced yet reoriented, to find Christ already displaced, waiting for us outside.

Evangelism, as "sending out," is now refocused. Rather than being sent out "with a message," the baptized are sent out to encounter others in all their blessings and suffering. The baptized are sent as the body of Christ but they also encounter the brokenness of Christ in the world. Thus, they encounter the body of Christ, particularly in those people who are suffering; for there, in the suffering of the neighbor, they encounter again, today, the cross of Jesus Christ. This refocusing suggests, of course, that the spread of the good news occurs not only through explicit, verbal proclamation of the word but through our lives as they are committed, engaged, conformed to the suffering in the world.

It is then of no small matter to evangelism that people are starving, that people are dying of HIV/AIDS, that there is still racial injustice here and in other parts of the world, that there is great material inequality, that there is violence (gun violence and sexual violence to name only two) hurting our communities. The "politics" of baptism (which Paul describes in Gal. 3:28, "there is no longer Jew or Greek, there is no longer slave or free, there is no longer male and female") and the "economics" of holy communion (that, as Paul admonishes us in 1 Cor. 11, there is enough for all) places the center at the edges—places us, as people of God, at the edges. "Bringing people to Jesus Christ" means being brought to Christ ourselves and taking our selves—our lives, our comforts, our dreams—to the edges where our suffering neighbor is calling out for help.

Perhaps it was this amazing discovery, that they could heal the suffering of the world, that made the seventy return from their mission with joy, "Lord, in your name even the demons submit to us" (Luke 10:17). You will remember the beginning of this passage from Luke 10:1-5.

> After this the Lord appointed seventy others and sent them on ahead of him in pairs to every town and place where he himself intended to go. He said to them, "The harvest is plentiful, but the laborers are few; therefore ask the Lord of the harvest to send out laborers into his harvest. Go on your way. See, I am sending you out like lambs into the midst of wolves. Carry no purse, no bag, no sandals; and greet no one on the road. Whatever house you enter, first say, 'Peace to this house!'"

The disciples were sent out with little provisions, not even sandals! This command can of course be read as the disciples' utter dependence on the word to nourish and care for them during their mission. It can be understood as the disciples' complete desire to be one with the people, renouncing all privilege. However, I believe this passage can also be read liturgically. When on holy ground, sandals were removed. As Moses stood before the burning bush, he was told to remove his sandals (Exod. 3). This ritual and respect for holy places has remained alive in many religions. In the Gospels, the disciples are sent out into countryside to announce that the dominion of God is near to you (Luke 10:9), *and* they are sent out without sandals. They are sent out, we could say, onto holy ground. They are sent out onto the holy ground of the world where God is, in fact, already waiting for them. They are sent out into the world, but this sending is not bridging any gaps between two realms, between "them and us," it is not reaching out to the "unreached," rather it is engaging a communion with all those waiting in despair and in hope.

In the parallel passage from Matthew 10, the disciples are instructed to proclaim the good news, cure the sick, raise the dead, cleanse the lepers, and cast out demons (Matt. 10:7-8). The proclamation consists in breaking down barriers, in the establishment of justice in the land, in the healing of the sick and the reinsertion of those suffering from stigmatized disease into communion with God and the community. The proclamation consists in the work of justice

and a radical communion—a real fellowship—with the infirmities of
the neighbor.

Christ and all the saints

When worship draws us toward the center, it draws us finally toward
Jesus Christ, crucified and risen. But it is now clearer that Christ is not
trapped in any of our words, no matter how eloquent, no matter how
theologically compelling; Christ is not trapped in any of our liturgies
or symbols no matter how beautifully celebrated. To be sure, all these
things—words, water, bread and wine, prayers and preaching—proclaim the promised presence of Christ to us (for here the infinite God
deigns to be contained in broken, finite things). Yet that same proclamation sends us out to share the water of life with the thirsty, food
with the hungry, justice for the oppressed and excluded. That is the
heart of worship—forming our lives in the pattern of proclamation of
Christ with us, inside, and Christ waiting for us, outside.

Another point we have sometimes missed in Luther's early writing
on the Lord's supper is that Luther almost never mentions "Christ"
without adding "and all the saints." Christ and the communion of
believers are inextricably linked. Incarnation and community are
inseparable. The neighbor and the believer are both caught up in the
incredible gift of God's continual revelation through word and sacraments. Through the participation in the sacrament of holy communion, we are made one with Christ and with all the saints in their
works, sufferings, and merit.[71] Union with Christ does not lead to
individualistic piety (Jesus and me) as has often happened in our
present-day practice. By insisting on communion in the suffering and
merit with all the saints, Luther gives no space for an individualist
religion concerned only with personal salvation. Many grains become
one bread means that we too become one with all the others.

This breaking open of the center—of our selves—becomes our
call. In the sacrament, faith is given as gift rather than as possession.

In the distribution of Christ's body and blood, faith is given. In the distribution of God, God conforms us to Christ in the assembly, and God conforms us to Christ in the suffering neighbor. And evangelism happens then, not as our work, but as God's work of real fellowship in the world.

The immediacy of the sacrament, of God's revelation, is expressed symbolically, in language and in gesture. One of the primary recommendations of the early regulations for Reformation churches (*Kirchenordnungen*) was that there always be a common chest for the poor.[72] After a lengthy chapter on the use and misuse of the mass (and instructions on how the mass should be enacted), Pastor Johannes Bugenhagen follows up with a chapter on the common chest. The line from the eucharist to the common chest, though not explicitly stated, is strongly suggested.[73] "All the trials (literally 'cries for help') of body and soul of our brothers [and sisters], whether rich or poor, should be mine."[74] We cannot truly share in holy communion without sharing in humanity's plight. However, now the correlation between the two is not "extrinsic" (that is, not a cause and effect, not "I do this in order to … or because of …") but rather is "living." The promise of God is living the liturgy in the pain of the world—at the edges. The symbolic language of the liturgy, the pattern of worship, is the language of faith and love, the language of communion with the other.

Through the eucharist (in the promise of forgiveness), we are made one with Christ and with the neighbor. The confrontation occurs in "being made one with." We are confronted in our self-centered tendencies whether they are self-justification, pride, individualism, self-gratification of religious emotions, or reason itself. Sin works through these different forms always isolating the individual from a restored communion with Christ and the neighbor.

For Luther, sin is strongly identified with rebellion against God and escape from human community. He considers those who are unwilling to be confronted by the sacrament to be people afraid of the world. They do not want to suffer "disfavor, harm, shame, or death although it is God's will that they be thus driven."[75] They do not want to share in the suffering to which forgiveness of sins calls them. They may be willing to pray in the liturgy but they minimize what beseeching entails. They may recognize the thanksgiving (the meaning of the Greek word *eucharistia*), but they ignore the sharing. Yet, the gift of faith that comes to us in word and sacrament is God reintegrating and re-creating a communion, not only between God and us but also between the neighbor and us. The eucharist "bursts open all the bolts and fetters of this perishing world of death."[76] The eucharist bursts open all the fetters and self-invented centers that impede communion.

The eucharist confronts us with a new language about the world, with a new order or law for life. Like the bread of life, we are broken and distributed; we share in the sufferings and the pain of Christ and in the sufferings and pain of the neighbor. The common chest set next to the eucharistic celebration is not duty or obligation, not discipline or self-mastery, but witnesses to our own suffering reality. The eucharist defines life as a continual involvement in the dying and rising of Christ that has no end until our bodily death and resurrection.

This confrontation with dying and rising in the eucharist is not merely an emotional or psychological drama. It has become far too easy to equate "awesome" religious emotion with a sense that we have "died," that is, that we have given something up for God. The dying of which Luther speaks is a concrete participation in the death of Christ, in the suffering of ourselves and others. This participation in Jesus' command, "Do this in remembrance of me" is not simply an inward act of the heart but an outward and public remembering.[77] The believer is sent into the world: "Go in peace. Serve the Lord!"

After words: being sent
Already in the writing of Justin Martyr (a Christian theologian of the second century), we read that there was a collection and a sharing

with the poor, with orphans and widows, with those in want because of sickness or other reason, and with those in prison and the visiting strangers. The needs of all, Justin writes, are addressed. But in this text from Justin, we read about another sending: everyone shares in the "eucharisterized" (consecrated) food, and then this consecrated food, bread and wine, is sent via the deacons to those absent. The "eucharisterized" food sent out became known as the *fermentum*.

In Justin, the "eucharisterized" bread and wine, the *fermentum*, sent to all who were absent and the gifts collected for the poor and the needy are both ways in which the liturgy is participating in the world. Later, the *fermentum* was sent out from the bishop's celebration at the main church to all the other churches in the region as a sign of the unity between the churches. But this sending did not have as its goal the establishment of the episcopal mass as the center; rather the sending was to be a sign of communion between all the churches. The eucharist was a ferment of union, of communion.

It is Luther who helps us make the connection between this *fermentum*, this eucharistic gesture, and evangelism. The *fermentum* sent out into the world, the body of Christ given to the world, is our own body, which we have become in the supper. We are the *fermentum* sent out from the liturgy. We are given to the world. We are sent out into the world as the body of Christ. But we are not sent out to bridge any gaps. We are not the "holy ones" who march out as Christian soldiers into the foreboding and hostile world.

We go out "in peace"—truly in peace—for this work, the work of evangelism, is not our doing. We go in peace because God has conformed us to Christ through the bath, the word, the meal, and even the suffering of our neighbor. It is not we who are going out into the world; it is not our reason, our goal, our ambition, our effort, our call that is sent out into the world to accomplish something. It is not by any effort or good work on our part that we are ever able to accomplish Christ's mission in the world. We are sent out to serve the Lord. We are sent, not merely as a servant commanded to accomplish a task or requirement, not as a servant dutifully obeying the master, nor in any self-righteous extension of ourselves. Instead, we are sent to encounter God as the abandoned man lying in the street near a heating duct, as the woman selling her body, as the addict stoned on the bench or in the bar, or as the single parent raising children without knowing from where the next check will come, and in all the less dramatic wounds and hurts of the neighbors we daily encounter.

Centripetal worship—worship that witnesses and draws us to the center, to Jesus Christ and the promise of his presence—forms us into a real fellowship and now sends us out as memory of a meal, as "eucharisterized" food, as leaven of comfort and joy, of peace and justice, within the human family. Isn't that evangelism in the world?

For reflection and discussion

1. How is the dynamic between "center" and "edges" presented in this chapter?

2. What does this redefinition mean for evangelism in your context?

3. Where do you see the mentality of "insider/outsider" operative in your local community?

4. How does Martin Luther's insistence on holy communion as "real fellowship" (rather than just individualistic piety) affect the ways in which we celebrate the Lord's supper?

5. Reflect back on all the chapters of this book. We began with the contrast between "centripetal worship" and worship that sends people away without recognizing the central things around which we gather: the forgiving and life-giving voice and presence of Christ in word and sacrament. Luther's reform of worship taught us how, with Christ at the center of worship, Christians can enjoy a variety of forms and languages in worship while rejecting any hint of works righteousness and sacrifice. Similarly, we learned that all music in worship calls people to the center, where Christ meets us with forgiveness and mercy. Drawn to that same center, people become not an audience to be entertained but participants, free to work for the sake of all who come. Finally, the Christ we encounter at the center of worship encounters us at the edges of the Christian assembly, in the world, with those in need, transforming our evangelism into true care for others. How has learning these things and conversing about them changed or strengthened your understanding of worship?

6. An old Christmas hymn encourages us to "Come and worship . . . the newborn king." This book has been an invitation to do the same. May angels sing that invitation in your ears throughout your life!

Contributors

DIRK G. LANGE is Assistant Professor of Christian Assembly at The Lutheran Theological Seminary at Philadelphia (LTSP), where he teaches liturgy and homiletics. A brother at Taizé for 19 years, Professor Lange was ordained in 2002. He was an active member of Renewing Worship project as a member of the editorial board for Daily Prayer. He has edited and contributed to an introduction to liturgy in honor of Gordon W. Lathrop, *Ordo: Bath, Word, Prayer, Table.* While a parish pastor in Atlanta, he received his doctorate at Emory University in 2005, writing on Martin Luther's eucharistic hermeneutics.

F. RUSSELL MITMAN is Conference Minister and President of Pennsylvania Southeast Conference of the United Church of Christ. He holds a Th.M. from Princeton Theological Seminary, where he wrote on Mercersburg Theology. He received a D.Min. in preaching from Chicago Theological Seminary. That work was enlarged and published as *Worship in the Shape of Scripture* (Cleveland: Pilgrim Press, 2001). In 2005 he edited for Pilgrim, *Immersed in the Splendor of God: Resources for Worship Renewal.* In the spring of 2007 a companion volume of liturgies for occasional services, *Blessed by the Presence of God*, will be published by Pilgrim. He has led many workshops on worship leadership and is a leader in the Philadelphia Liturgical Institute.

MARK MUMMERT is the seminary musician at LTSP. He is a composer of Setting One of Holy Communion in *Evangelical Lutheran Worship* and served on the training team for the introduction of the book of worship to the synods of the church. The chapter in this volume began as lectures for the Church Music Symposium in Gothenburg, Sweden (October 2006), and the "Breaking Bread, Breaking Boundaries" Worship Conference of the Evangelical Lutheran Church in Canada (July 2005).

MELINDA QUIVIK is Assistant Professor of Christian Assembly at LTSP, where she teaches courses in liturgy and homiletics. A graduate of LTSP, she served pastorates for eight years in Montana and Minnesota. She earned her doctorate at the Graduate Theological Union in Berkeley, California, writing on liturgical aesthetics and the funeral rite. She contributed to the Worship Matters series with *A Christian Funeral: Witness to the Resurrection*, and was active in the Renewing Worship project of the ELCA.

TIMOTHY J. WENGERT is the Ministerium of Pennsylvania Professor of Reformation History and Lutheran Confessions at LTSP. He served pastorates in Minnesota and Wisconsin before being called to the Seminary in 1989. He has written extensively on Philip Melanchthon and other Reformation topics. In 2000, a new translation of *The Book of Concord* (Fortress, 2000) appeared, which he and Robert Kolb of Concordia Seminary, St. Louis edited. His widely used translation of the Small Catechism from that project appeared already in 1994 and was included in *Evangelical Lutheran Worship*. With Gordon Lathrop, he co-authored *Christian Assembly* (Fortress, 2004), and has most recently published a commentary on the Formula of Concord, *A Formula for Parish Practice* (Eerdmans, 2006).

Bibliography

Appiah, Kwame Anthony. *Cosmopolitanism: Ethics in a World of Strangers*. New York: W. W. Norton, 2006.

Bacher, Robert, and Kenneth Inskeep, *Chasing Down a Rumor: The Death of Mainline Denominations*. Minneapolis: Augsburg Fortress, 2005.

Bliese, Richard H., and Craig Van Gelder, eds. *The Evangelizing Church: A Lutheran Contribution*. Minneapolis: Fortress, 2005.

Dawn, Marva J. *A Royal Waste of Time: The Splendor of Worshiping God and Being Church for the World*. Grand Rapids, MI: Eerdmans, 1999.

Haemig, Mary Jane. "Elisabeth Cruciger (1500?–1535): The Case of the Disappearing Hymn Writer." *Sixteenth Century Journal* 32 (2001), 21–44.

Janz, Denis, ed. *Three Reformation Catechisms: Catholic, Anabaptist, Lutheran*. Lewiston, NY: Mellen, 1982.

Kelley, Tina. "Now in the Recovery Room, Music for Hearts to Heal By." *New York Times*, August 28, 2006.

Kolb, Robert, and Timothy J. Wengert, eds. *The Book of Concord*. Minneapolis: Fortress, 2000.

Lange, Dirk, and Dwight W. Vogel, eds. *Ordo: Bath, Word, Prayer, Table. A Liturgical Primer in Honor of Gordon W. Lathrop.* Akron, OH: OSL Publications, 2006.

Lathrop, Gordon W. *Holy Things: A Liturgical Theology.* Minneapolis: Augsburg Fortress, 1993.

Lathrop, Gordon. *The Pastor: A Spirituality.* Minneapolis: Fortress, 2006.

Levitin, Daniel J. *This Is Your Brain on Music: The Science of a Human Obsession.* New York: Dutton, 2006.

Lindberg, Carter. *Beyond Charity: Reformation Initiatives for the Poor.* Minneapolis: Fortress, 1993.

Luther, Martin. *Luther's Works* (American edition), Jarislav Pelikan and Helmut Lehmann, eds., 55 vols. Philadelphia: Fortress, and St. Louis: Concordia, 1955–1986.

Meuser, Fred. *Luther the Preacher.* Minneapolis: Augsburg, 1983.

Olin, John C. *The Catholic Reformation: Savonarola to Ignatius Loyola: Reform in the Church 1495–1540.* New York: Harper & Row, 1969.

Postman, Neil. *Amusing Ourselves to Death.* New York: Penguin, 1985.

Ramshaw, Gail. *Liturgical Language: Keeping It Metaphoric, Making It Inclusive.* Collegeville, MN: Liturgical Press, 1996.

Saliers, Donald and Emily. *A Song to Sing, a Life to Live: Reflections on Music As Spiritual Practice.* San Francisco: Jossey-Bass, 2005.

Schneiders, Sandra. *The Revelatory Text: Interpreting the New Testament as Sacred Scripture.* Collegeville, MN: Liturgical Press, 1999.

Senn, Frank C. *Christian Liturgy: Catholic and Evangelical.* Minneapolis: Fortress Press, 1997.

Vogel, Dwight W., ed. *Primary Sources of Liturgical Theology: A Reader.* Collegeville, MN: The Liturgical Press, 2000.

Warden, Michael D., ed. *Experience God in Worship.* Loveland, CO: Group Publishing Inc., 2000.

Wengert, Timothy J., and Gordon W. Lathrop. *Christian Assembly: Marks of the Church in a Pluralistic Age*. Minneapolis: Fortress, 2004.

Wengert, Timothy J., ed. *Harvesting Martin Luther's Reflections on Theology, Ethics, and the Church*. Grand Rapids, MI: Eerdmans, 2004.

Westermeyer, Paul. *Let the People Sing: Hymn Tunes in Perspective*. Chicago: GIA Publications, 2005.

With One Voice. Minneapolis: Augsburg Fortress, 1995.

Notes

Foreword

1. This foreword is based upon remarks Dr. Mitman made at The Lutheran Theological Seminary at Philadelphia as a response to Prof. Timothy J. Wengert's speech on "Centripetal Worship."

2. Gail Ramshaw, *Liturgical Language: Keeping It Metaphoric, Making It Inclusive* (Collegeville, MN: Liturgical Press, 1996), 10.

3. Marva J. Dawn, *A Royal Waste of Time: The Splendor of Worshiping God and Being Church for the World* (Grand Rapids, MI: Eerdmans, 1999), 158.

4. Frank C. Senn, *Christian Liturgy: Catholic and Evangelical* (Minneapolis: Fortress Press, 1997), 646.

5. Neil Postman, *Amusing Ourselves to Death* (New York: Penguin, 1985).

Chapter 1

6. This and the following chapter were first delivered in November 2006 at The Lutheran Theological Seminary at Philadelphia.

7. Gordon Lathrop, "Church Is Assembly," in idem and Timothy J. Wengert, *Christian Assembly: Marks of the Church in a Pluralistic Age* (Minneapolis: Fortress, 2004), 14.

8. See Gordon Lathrop, "Church Is Assembly," in idem and Wengert, *Christian Assembly*, passim.

9. Helmar Junghans, "Luther on Worship," in *Harvesting Martin Luther's Reflections on Theology, Ethics, and the Church*, ed. Timothy J. Wengert (Grand Rapids, MI: Eerdmans, 2004), 207–225.

10. For a description of late-medieval preaching, see John W. O'Malley, "Luther the Preacher," in *The Martin Luther Quincentennial*, ed. Gerhard Dünnhaupt (Detroit: Wayne State University Press, 1985), 3–16.

11. Dietrich Kolde, *Mirror for Christians (1480)*, in *Three Reformation Catechisms: Catholic, Anabaptist, Lutheran,* ed. Denis Janz (Lewiston, NY: Mellen, 1982), 96–97, 116–117.

12. John C. Olin, *The Catholic Reformation: Savonarola to Ignatius Loyola: Reform in the Church 1495–1540* (New York: Harper & Row, 1969), 16–26. Of course, people *watched* the mass with far more regularity. It was just the reception that was far rarer than today.

13. Dirk Lange, "The Didache: Liturgy Redefining Life," *Worship* 78 (2004), 203–225.

14. See page 70, and also Dirk Lange, "Eating, Drinking, Sending: Reflections on the Juxtaposition of Law and Event in the Eucharist," in *Ordo: Bath, Word, Prayer, Table. A Liturgical Primer in Honor of Gordon W. Lathrop,* ed. Dirk Lange and Dwight W. Vogel (Akron, OH: OSL Publications, 2006), 84–99.

15. Gordon Lathrop, *The Pastor: A Spirituality* (Minneapolis: Fortress, 2006), 27–28.

Chapter 2

16. *On the Babylonian Captivity of the Church* (1520), in *Luther's Works* 36:3–126.

17. Transubstantiation is the doctrine that, although the qualities of bread and wine remained (called "accidents" in Aristotelian language of the time), the essence (called "substance") were changed into Christ's body and blood. Lutherans confess that Christ's body and blood are truly present with the bread and wine, but they do not pretend to explain how this occurs.

18. Later, in the Apology [defense] of the Augsburg Confession, article XIII, its author, Philip Melanchthon (Luther's colleague in Wittenberg and chief drafter of the Augsburg Confession), could imagine circumstances under which ordination especially could once again be numbered among the sacraments. Only as more recent liturgical scholars have rediscovered confirmation's connection to baptism has it been pulled back into baptism's orbit so that today's Lutherans say similar things about it. The anointing of the sick, too, has also become in recent times a beautiful setting for the word, rather than a threat to the dying.

19. Martin Luther, *Marriage Booklet* (1529), in *The Book of Concord*, ed. Robert Kolb and Timothy J. Wengert (Minneapolis: Fortress, 2000), 368–369.

20. Helmar Junghans, "Luther on Worship," in *Harvesting Martin Luther's Reflections on Theology, Ethics, and the Church*, ed. Timothy J. Wengert (Grand Rapids, MI: Eerdmans, 2004), 207–225.

21. For more about Luther's preaching, see Fred Meuser, *Luther the Preacher* (Minneapolis: Augsburg, 1983).

22. See *The Martin Luther Christmas Book*, ed. Roland H. Bainton (Philadelphia: Muhlenberg Press, 1948), 38.

23. See Thomas Schattauer, ed., *Inside Out* (Minneapolis: Fortress, 1999).

24. In a sermon on Colossians 3:12-17 in *Sermons of Martin Luther*, trans. John Lenker, 8 vols. (Reprint: Grand Rapids: Baker, 1989), 5: 89–91.

25. Mary Jane Haemig, "Elisabeth Cruciger (1500?–1535): The Case of the Disappearing Hymn Writer," *Sixteenth Century Journal* 32 (2001), 21–44.

26. Author's translation of a portion of the final stanza.

27. Gordon Lathrop uses this pithy description of the Christian *ordo* (reading and preaching on God's word, celebrating the Lord's supper and baptism, and prayers and praise) in, among other places, "The Marks of the Church in the Liturgy," in idem and Timothy J. Wengert, *Christian Assembly: Marks of the Church in a Pluralistic Age* (Minneapolis: Fortress, 2004), 46–47.

28. Teachers and bishops of the ancient church, active in the fourth and fifth centuries.

29. Joachim Mörlin, *Historia Welcher gestalt sich die Osiandrische schwermerey im lande zu Preussen erhaben, vnd wie dieselbige verhandelt ist, mit allen actis beschrieben* ([Magdeburg: Michael Lotter], 1554), R 3v – R 4r, author's translation.

30. An *adiaphoron* (plural: adiaphora) is a Greek ethical term, especially used by Lutheran Christians since the time of the Reformation, to denote matters in which people cannot differentiate between right and wrong or good and bad. They are sometimes called "indifferent matters," a slightly incorrect translation of the Latin equivalent of adiaphora, *indifferentia* (literally, undifferentiated matters).

31. Ambrose, bishop of Milan, "Veni redemptor gentium" ("Savior of the Nations, Come," *Evangelical Lutheran Worship* #263). Stanza three could be translated literally: "Proceeding from his bedchamber [woman's bedroom, *thalamus*], queenly court of modesty, Giant of twin substance, eager so that he may run the race." Ambrose calls Jesus the "Gigas," or giant, of pagan mythology.

32. I thank Gordon Lathrop for pointing out this connection to me.

33. Timothy J. Wengert, "Luther and Melanchthon on Consecrated Communion Wine (Eisleben 1542–43)," *Lutheran Quarterly* 15 (2001), 24–42.

Chapter 3

34. Some translations, such as *Today's English Version* suggest that the musician played a harp.

35. Tina Kelley, "Now in the Recovery Room, Music for Hearts to Heal By," *New York Times*, August 28, 2006.

36. Daniel J. Levitin, *This Is Your Brain on Music: The Science of a Human Obsession* (New York: Dutton, 2006), 137.

37. Levitin, *This Is Your Brain on Music*, 172.

38. The minnesingers were guilds of musicians singing in German and traveling from court to court in the twelfth through fourteenth centuries. Their principal song, called "*minnelied*" (German for love song) was in bar form (AAB) in which the opening phrases (*stollen*) are repeated and then the song is concluded (*abgesang*) with new material, the last phrase often borrowing from some material from the opening phrases. In the fifteenth and sixteenth centuries, Meistersingers replaced the minnesingers, and Wagner's opera "Die Meistersinger von Nürnberg" chronicles one such singing competition of these traveling musicians.

39. Paul Westermeyer, *Let the People Sing: Hymn Tunes in Perspective* (Chicago: GIA Publications, 2005), 22.

Chapter 4

40. For another view of this proposed trajectory for church membership please refer to Robert Bacher and Kenneth Inskeep, *Chasing Down a Rumor: The Death of Mainline Denominations* (Minneapolis: Augsburg Fortress, 2005), 84: "The accepted wisdom is that the mainline denominations are weak and getting weaker. It is our view, however, that mainline denominations have never really been that strong, despite brief appearance at center stage from about 1920 through the 1950s. Mainline denominations have *always* been somewhat distant and remote from the heartfelt religion of regular people, so this is nothing new."

41. Leonard Sweet, "A New Reformation: Re-Creating Worship for a Postmodern World," in *Experience God in Worship*, ed. Michael D. Warden (Loveland, CO: Group Publishing Inc., 2000), 173. Sweet uses the word "postmodern" to denote intuitive approaches to knowledge as opposed to the "modern" emphasis on objective knowing. The postmodern person, Sweet claims, wants emotive, personal, and authentic experience in community with others.

42. Sweet, "A New Reformation," 180.

43. Gordon W. Lathrop, *Holy Things: A Liturgical Theology* (Minneapolis: Augsburg Fortress, 1993), 5.

44. Kwame Anthony Appiah, *Cosmopolitanism: Ethics in a World of Strangers* (New York: W. W. Norton, 2006), 84. I am indebted to Gordon Lathrop for alerting me to this book.

45. Eugene Brand, "Lutheran Liturgical Renewal: The Pastoral Motif," in *Bulletin of the Martin Luther Colloquium 1975 in Honor of Donald R. Heiges: Luther, Worship and Liturgical Renewal* 56/1 (February 1976), 28. Held in the ELCA Archives' ILCW papers in Chicago.

46. Brand, "Lutheran Liturgical Renewal," 30.

47. Here and elsewhere in this chapter, "Sunday morning" denotes the regular weekly assembly, whether it occurs precisely on Sunday or not.

48. Sandra Schneiders, *The Revelatory Text: Interpreting the New Testament as Sacred Scripture* (Collegeville, MN: Liturgical Press, 1999), 82. With the term "hermeneutical dialectic," Schneiders is describing the alternating sides in the development of scripture.

49. "Historic models are never finally determinative." Lathrop, *Holy Things*, 6.

50. At baptism: "Immerse in the name of the Father and of the Son and of the Holy Spirit in flowing water—if, on the other hand, you should not have flowing water, immerse in other water; and if you are not able in cold, immerse in warm; and if you should not have either, pour out water onto the head three times in the name of Father and Son and holy Spirit." Aaron Milavec, ed., *The Didache* (The Liturgical Press, 2003), 19. Over the bread and wine: "We give you thanks, our Father, for the holy vine of your servant David which you revealed to us through your servant Jesus. To you [is] the glory forever." *The Didache*, 23.

51. Justin Martyr, "First Apology," in *Springtime of the Liturgy: Liturgical Texts of the First Four Centuries*, ed. Lucien Deiss (Collegeville, MN: The Liturgical Press, 1979), 93–94.

52. *With One Voice* (Minneapolis: Augsburg Fortress, 1995), 6–7.

53. Appiah, *Cosmopolitanism*, 134–135.

54. For a good overview of liturgical renewal see James F. Puglisi, ed., *Liturgical Renewal as a Way to Christian* Unity (Collegeville, MN: The Liturgical Press, 2005); or John Fenwick and Bryan Spinks, *Worship in Transition: The Liturgical Movement in the Twentieth Century* (New York: Continuum, 1995). For historical background, see Marcel Metzger, *History of the Liturgy: The Major Stages* (Collegeville, MN: The Liturgical Press, 1997).

55. In contrast, "traditions [plural] are the limited formulations distilled from this flood of Christian life"—Schneiders, 91 n. 17. This is Schneiders' paraphrase of George Tavard, "Tradition in Theology: A Methodological Approach," in *Perspectives on Scripture and Tradition*, 114–124. Please note that the distinction between "traditions" and "Tradition" has often been used in the ecumenical movement to designate a slightly different formulation than Schneiders is articulating here through Tavard's work.

56. Schneiders, *The Revelatory Text*, 78.

57. The exceptions to having the ordained preach and pray at table have been in places where the need for pastors is greater than the supply. There, the churches have trained and licensed lay persons to provide for the congregations' needs. The church's commitment to the public office should never diminish the dedication and faithfulness of such persons.

58. See chapter 3 for Mark Mummert's approach to this issue.

Chapter 5

59. *Sermons on John 3–4* (1538–1540), in *Luther's Works* 22:520, here commenting on John 4:9.

60. *Luther's Works* 35:80–81.

61. Martin Luther to Georg Buchholzer in Berlin, from a letter dated 4/5 December 1539, in *Luthers Werke: Kritische Gesamtausgabe: Briefwechsel*, 18 vols. (Weimar, Germany: H. Böhlau, 1930–1985) 8: 624–626.

62. Unlike other places in his writings, Luther uses the word *mass* in a wholly positive sense as the designation for the service of holy communion.

63. *Luther's Works* 35:49–73, written in 1519.

64. *Luther's Works* 35:58.

65. *Luther's Works* 35:58.

66. *Luther's Works* 35:68.

67. *Luther's Works* 35:68–69.

68. J. Paul Rajashekar, "Navigating Difficult Questions," in *The Evangelizing Church: A Lutheran Contribution*, ed. Richard H. Bliese and Craig Van Gelder (Minneapolis: Fortress, 2005), 102.

69. John F. Hoffmeyer, "The Missional Trinity," *Dialog*, 41 (2001), 109.

70. Hoffmeyer, "The Missional Trinity," 110–111.

71. *Luther's Works* 35:60.

72. Johannes Bugenhagen, *Kirchenordnung für die Stadt Braunschweig* (Wolfenbüttel, Germany: J. Zwizler, 1885). The Braunschweig church order of 1528, written by Wittenberg chief pastor Johannes Bugenhagen, was the first and formative model for all the later church orders. See Carter Lindberg, *Beyond Charity: Reformation Initiatives for the Poor* (Minneapolis: Fortress, 1993), 142.

73. Bugenhagen, *Kirchenordnung*, 153–270.

74. Bugenhagen, *Kirchenordnung*, 270.

75. *Luther's Works* 35:57.

76. Peter Brunner, "Divine Service in the Church," in *Primary Sources of Liturgical Theology: A Reader*, ed. Dwight W. Vogel (Collegeville, MN: The Liturgical Press, 2000), 209.

77. *Psalm 111 Interpreted* (1530), in *Luther's Works* 13:365–366.